Contents

SOUPS

VEGETABLE DISHES

VEGETABLE COMBINATIONS

NUT DISHES

RICE, MACARONI, ETC.

CROQUETTES

TIMBALES AND PATTIES

SAUCES

EGG DISHES

CHEESE RECIPES

Measures

1 tablespoon = 3 teaspoons
4 tablespoons = 1/4 cup
1 cup = 250 ml
1 pint = 500 ml
1 quart = 0.95 L
1 gallon = 3.8 L

1 teaspoon = 5 ml
1 tablespoon or 1/2 fluid ounce =15 ml
1 fluid ounce or 1/8 cup= 30 ml
1/4 cup or 2 fluid ounces =60 ml
1/3 cup= 80 ml
1/2 cup or 4 fluid ounces=120 ml
2/3 cup=160 ml
3/4 cup or 6 fluid ounces=180 ml
1 cup or 8 fluid ounces or half a pint= 240 ml
2 cups or 1 pint or 16 fluid ounces =475 ml
4 cups or 2 pints or 1 quart = 950 ml

1 ounce = 28 g
4 ounces or 1/4 pound =113 g
1/3 pound=150 g
8 ounces or 1/2 pound =230 g
2/3 pound =300 g
12 ounces or 3/4 pound =340 g
1 pound or 16 ounces =450 g
2 pounds= 900 g

SOUPS

Most clear soups can be greatly improved in colour by using a small quantity of vegetable soup browning, or caramel. Do not overdo it, however, as the flavour is not pleasant when too pronounced. All cream soups should be cooked in a double boiler.

VEGETABLE STOCK

Few meat stocks have of themselves more flavour than vegetable stock, that is, the water in which vegetables have cooked. The water in which rice, onions, leeks, celery, beans, cabbage, etc., have boiled is valuable in Vegetarian cookery, and the wise cook will use it in many ways to enhance the flavours of soups and sauces.

A SIMPLE CONSOMMÉ OR STOCK

A simple way of preparing a rich, clear consommé is to wash well ½ cup of German lentils, drain them and toss them for ten minutes in a saucepan in which 1 tablespoon of butter has been melted. Then pour on them 5 cups of cold water, set them over a hot fire, and let them boil rapidly about half an hour only. Drain, and strain through a fine cloth, and return to a clean saucepan with 1 bay leaf, 1 slice of onion, 2 cloves, and ½ teaspoon of celery seed; simmer slowly for fifteen minutes, season with salt and pepper, and add a little sherry if liked.

If the lentils are cooked longer, it will make a cloudy soup, which will be stronger but not clear.

CLEAR BOUILLON OR CONSOMMÉ

There are various vegetable extracts in the market which, when diluted, make delicious stock, or clear soup. If these are not available, a clear vegetable broth may be made as follows:

Wash 3 cups of any dried beans or lentils, and put them to soak in a covered earthenware dish with 10 cups of water for twelve hours or so. Then empty with that same water into a kettle, and let come slowly to the boiling point, skim frequently, and do not let it actually boil. When clear, and there seems no further need of skimming, add 1 cup each of cut onions, carrots, turnips, 1 tablespoon of parsley, 1 tablespoon of salt, 1 clove of garlic, and 1 teaspoon of thyme, etc., 1 tablespoon of celery seed, and 1 bay leaf.

Let boil up once, and then place on the back of the stove to barely simmer for two hours; then strain through a fine sieve, and a good broth is made. The beans, etc., can be utilised in a deep pie, or with brown or white sauce in crust cups, in a curry, or many other ways.

To make this into a strong, clear soup put 2 tablespoons of butter in a saucepan, and when melted add ½ cup each of chopped onions, carrots, turnips, and celery, 2 cloves, and a bit of parsley; fry until somewhat browned, then cover with 6 cups of the broth, and let simmer very quietly for two hours. Skim often, drain, let cool, remove any grease from the top, and to clarify add to it, when cold, the slightly beaten yolk of 1 egg and the whites of 3, then set over a hot fire and stir vigorously, watching for the first sign of boiling. At this, remove to a place where it cannot even simmer, but will be warm for half an hour, and strain through a fine, clean cloth. A wineglass of sherry may be added if to be served in cups.

CREAM OF ARTICHOKE

Scrape and slice enough Jerusalem artichokes to make 2 cups, and cover them with cold water. Let them stand for fifteen or twenty minutes, and put them in a saucepan with 2 quarts of cold water or milk, or 1 quart of each, and let them cook for an hour or until thoroughly soft. Now rub them through a sieve with 2 cups of the stock in which they cooked, and return to the fire. When boiling add 1 tablespoon of butter and 1 of flour, rubbed together, and 1 teaspoon of salt and 1 saltspoon of pepper, and cook about ten minutes before adding 2 cups of hot milk, or 1 cup of milk and 1 cup of cream. Stir well and let boil up once before serving. A teaspoon of chopped parsley or chives improves the appearance and taste of almost any cream soup.

CREAM OF ARTICHOKE WITH NASTURTIUMS

Make the plain cream of artichoke soup as in preceding recipe, and add before straining 1 handful of nasturtium leaves and blossoms; or, instead, add 1 tablespoon of these, finely minced, to the soup before serving.

PLAIN BEAN SOUP

Wash 2 cups of any sort of dried beans and soak twelve hours or more in cold water. Before using, strain them and cover with 8 cups of cold water. Put over the fire and let cook gently for four hours, then rub them through a sieve into their own stock, season with 1 tablespoon of salt and ½ teaspoon of pepper and 1 tablespoon of butter, and let them cook ten minutes longer. Serve with half-inch squares of toast in the tureen.

ASPARAGUS SOUP

Use 1 can of asparagus, cut off the tips, and lay them aside. Cut up the stalks, cover with 4 cups of cold milk (or use half water and half milk), and let cook slowly in a double boiler for half an hour; then strain, pressing the asparagus well to extract the flavour. Return to the saucepan, add 1 teaspoon of sugar, 1 tablespoon of butter, into which 1 teaspoon of flour has been made smooth, season generously with salt and pepper, add the asparagus tips, 1 cup of milk, and, just before serving, 1 tablespoon of whipped cream. A tablespoon of minced onion fried for ten minutes in butter is sometimes added to the stalks while cooking.

BARLEY AND TOMATO SOUP

Cook 1 can of tomatoes and 1 chopped Spanish onion together for fifteen minutes, then rub through a wire sieve; add 3 tablespoons of pearl barley, 1 tablespoon of butter, some pepper and salt, and cook for one hour, until the barley is soft. Re-season before serving.

BLACK BEAN SOUP

Soak 2 cups of beans for twelve hours or more, and then drain them and put into 8 cups of cold water; add 3 whole cloves, 3 whole allspice, and 3 whole peppers, salt well and boil gently for two hours, rub through sieve, and reheat. Mix 1 tablespoon of thickening flour, and 1 tablespoon of butter and water, and stir into the soup at boiling point; season afresh and pour into a tureen in which are placed, neatly sliced, 1 hard-boiled egg and half a dozen seeded slices of lemon. This soup is improved by adding 1 wineglass of sherry, or one may substitute for it a few drops of Tomato Chutney or Worcestershire sauce.

BELGIAN SOUP

Take 4 cups of diced turnips and put them in a saucepan with 2 tablespoons of butter, and stir for ten minutes over a slow fire; then stir in 2 cups of water, 2 teaspoons of brown sugar, and plenty of pepper and salt, and let simmer for another ten minutes; add 2 cups of milk thickened with 1 tablespoon of flour, let boil up, stirring constantly, and serve with croutons.

BROWN BEAN SOUP

Take 1 cup of brown beans and ½ cup of German lentils, wash well and put in a saucepan with plenty of cold water, 2 or 3 chopped onions, 1 stalk of celery, 1 bay leaf, and simmer together for three hours, then strain. If a thin soup is wanted, do not press any of the pulp through the strainer, but if it is liked somewhat thick, do so. Return the strained soup to the saucepan and thicken with 1 teaspoon of thickening flour. This is now delicious soup stock, and can be served plain, or varied by adding peas, diced carrots, spaghetti, a few drops of sauce, a little sherry, tomato catsup, or curry powder. Season well with salt and pepper before serving.

RED BEAN SOUP

Soak for 8 hours or more 2 cups of red beans, then put them in a large saucepan containing 8 cups of cold water, 1 cup of milk, and 2 onions halved, each having 4 cloves stuck in it. Let cook for two hours, then press through a sieve, reheat, adding just before serving 1 wineglass of claret and fresh seasoning of salt and pepper. 1 hard-boiled egg chopped fine is an improvement to this soup.

LIMA BEAN CREAM SOUP

Soak 2 cups of dried lima beans for several hours and then put them in a saucepan with 1 cup of cold water and 1 cup of milk and let them cook for two hours, adding salt when they have partly cooked. Put 1 tablespoon of butter in a frying pan, and when melted add 1 onion chopped fine. Let cook slowly until browned, then scrape the contents of the frying pan into the saucepan containing the beans, and add 1 tablespoon of tomato catsup or chutney and press all through a sieve, and re-season before serving. If liked a little thick, use 1 tablespoon of flour, made smooth in ½ cup of milk or cream, to thicken. A tablespoon of whipped cream in the tureen is always an improvement to a cream soup.

DUTCH CABBAGE SOUP

Make exactly like Cockie-Leekie soup, using the water in which a cabbage has boiled for stock and adding ½ cup of finely chopped cabbage instead of using any of the barley to return to the strained soup. Those who like caraway seed will enjoy the addition of 1 teaspoon of these to the soup. If used, add them with the chopped cabbage after the other seasoning has been removed.

CREAM OF CARROT AND ONION

Take 2 cups of grated carrot and 1 chopped onion and fry for ten minutes with 1 tablespoon of butter and then cover with 4 cups of cold water and let boil. Add salt and pepper and in twenty minutes 1 cup of milk in which 1 tablespoon of flour has been dissolved.

CALCUTTA BISQUE

Put 1 cup of tomato pulp in a saucepan and with it 1 bay leaf. When hot add to it 1 saltspoon of soda, and as it foams stir slowly into it 3 or 4 cups of milk, 1 teaspoon of curry powder, 1 teaspoon of butter, and 1 saltspoon of salt. Let boil up once and serve with croutons.

The water in which rice has boiled or any vegetable stock may be substituted for milk and the soda then omitted.

CREAM OF CORN

Put 1 quart of milk and 1 can of corn in a double boiler and let boil; mix 1 teaspoon of butter and 1 of cornstarch or potato-flour together, and add to the corn; season with salt and pepper, and stir for one minute; then press through a sieve and add 1 tablespoon of minced green peppers.

CANTON STEW

Put 2 cups of finely shredded cabbage in enough water to boil and let cook slowly until tender, which should be in about three quarters of an hour. When the cabbage has been cooking half an hour, add a cup of milk, and when it is nearly done put in 2 cups of milk; let boil up once, then season with salt, black pepper, and pour in a hot tureen, in which should be laid 1 teaspoon of butter. Those who like oyster crackers served in or with milk stews can use them with this soup which greatly resembles an oyster stew in flavour.

CARROT BROTH

Scrape and cut 3 or 4 large carrots (or more of the small French sort) in eighths lengthwise and boil them until tender. Put 2 tablespoons of butter in a saucepan, and when melted add 1 scant half cup of oatmeal to it, putting in 1 tablespoon at a time and stirring carefully with a wooden spoon until all the butter is taken up; then put in 1 ladle of stock in which the carrots have been cooked, and continue stirring; then another ladle of stock, and so on until a cup and a half of stock has been added during ten minutes' slow cooking. Now put in another cup of stock and let cook ten minutes; then, as the soup will be getting too thick, add another cup of stock and so on, thinning the soup with additional stock until the oatmeal is thoroughly cooked. If Quaker Oats is used, the soup will only have to cook about forty minutes, and it is best to strain it before serving; fine Scotch meal will take longer, but does not need to be strained and thickens somewhat better.

When the soup is half cooked add 1 teaspoon of salt, 1 saltspoon of pepper, and a dash of nutmeg. (Serve the carrots with a plain sauce or warm them up next day in some of the ways mentioned under Carrots.)

CREAM OF CARROTS

Put 2 cups of grated carrot with 1 pint (2 cups) of cold water in a double boiler, and when heated add 2 tablespoons of butter and 1 teaspoon of sugar. Let cook for an hour, then add ½ cup of stale bread crumbs and 2 cups of water, and let cook half an hour longer. Rub the contents of the double boiler through a fine sieve, add 1½ cups of hot milk, 1 tablespoon of salt and a saltspoon of pepper, and return to the boiler. Beat 2 egg-yolks in ½ cup of milk, and when the soup boils again stir them into it. Stir hard for one minute and serve.

CREAM OF CHEESE

Put 1 quart (or 4 cups) of milk in a double boiler, and put with it ¾ of a cup of grated cheese, 1 teaspoon of grated onion, 1 teaspoon of some piquant sauce, ¼ teaspoon of salt, a dash of cayenne pepper, and 1 tablespoon of flour and 1 of butter rubbed together. Stir until smooth, then beat the yolks of 2 eggs with 2 tablespoons of milk, put in the tureen, and pour the boiling soup over them, stirring during the process. Add a little salt and serve with croutons.

CREAM OF CURRY

Put 1 quart (or 4 cups) of milk in a double boiler with 1 onion with 4 cloves stuck in it, and when hot thicken it with 1 tablespoon of thickening flour rubbed smooth with 1 tablespoon of butter; add 2 tablespoons of boiled rice, and 1 hard-boiled egg chopped fine, and 2 teaspoons (more if liked) of curry powder or paste. Remove the onion and serve with croutons. One tablespoon of chopped chives or pimentos is an addition to the soup.

CREAM OF CAULIFLOWER

Take a good-sized cauliflower, and let it soak in cold water, which is slightly salted, for half an hour; then drain it and put it, head upwards, in a saucepan which is not over large, and let it cook for half an hour *uncovered*. Put in a double boiler 1 quart of milk (4 cups), 1 onion and 1 bay leaf, and let them cook together while the cauliflower is boiling. Drain the cauliflower when done, and reserve ½ cup of the little sprays which form the head, mash the remainder in a wooden bowl, and add to it 2 cups of the stock in which it boiled and put in with the boiling milk; stir well, and let cook five minutes, then put through a sieve and return to the fire with a thickening of 1 tablespoon of flour rubbed together with 1 tablespoon of butter, season lightly with salt and pepper and a dash of nutmeg, add the ½ cup of cauliflower as a garnish, and let cook ten minutes more before serving. A tablespoon of whipped cream is an addition if added at the last.

CHESTNUT SOUP

Peel and blanch 1 quart of Italian chestnuts and chop them fine, then boil for half an hour in 2 quarts of water. Strain the chestnuts and crush them to fine pulp in a mortar, and gradually stir on this 1 quart of the stock in which the chestnuts cooked, and then rub all through a sieve. Return to the fire in a saucepan with 1 cup of bread crumbs, 1 tablespoon of salt, and 1 saltspoon of pepper. Cook for half an hour, then strain again, and add 2 cups of milk and a grating of nutmeg, and 1 tablespoon of browned butter, and reheat to boiling point.

CREAM OF CELERY

Wash and scrape and cut into half-inch pieces what will make 1 cup of celery; put it into 1 quart of boiling salted water and cook for nearly an hour or until very soft, then mash it in the water in which it was boiled. Put 1 teaspoon of chopped onion, 2 bay leaves, some mace, and 2 cloves into 2 cups of milk, let simmer for ten minutes, and add it to the celery pulp. Now press through a sieve and return to the double boiler in which the milk was cooked. Melt 1 tablespoon of butter and blend it with 1 tablespoon of flour until smooth, and stir it into the boiling soup; then season with salt and pepper. Boil five minutes and strain into a hot tureen in which a pat of butter and 1 tablespoon of whipped cream have been put. The addition of 1 tablespoon of chopped chives is an improvement to the appearance and taste, or parsley may be used if preferred.

CREAM OF CHESTNUT

Shell and blanch and cut in quarters 2 cups (1 pound) of Italian chestnuts and cover them with 2 cups of boiling water. Add 1 slice of onion (or a drop of onion juice extract), ¼ cup of chopped celery (or 1 teaspoon celery seed), 1 bay leaf, 1 sprig of parsley, and 1 saltspoon of paprika. Cover and boil until the chestnuts are tender,— about half an hour. Then grind in a mortar, or press through a colander or vegetable mill, and add 1 quart (4 cups) of milk, and 1 tablespoon of butter and 1 of flour rubbed together, and cook for three minutes; then add 1 teaspoon of salt, and press all through a fine sieve and reheat before serving.

FLORENTINE SOUP

Melt 2 tablespoons of butter in a saucepan, and put into it ¾ of a cup of finely chopped onions and stir over a moderate heat about five minutes and then add 2 full cups of very thinly sliced turnips; stir these with the onions for another five minutes and then add 2 tablespoons of flour and gradually add 2 pints of boiled milk mixing all well together; watch it till it boils and then let simmer gently, stirring frequently during twenty minutes or half an hour, until the onions are quite soft. Then add 2 more cups of milk, and when this boils add 1 cup of tomato puree (either canned tomato soup or canned tomatoes), or 1½ cups of sliced fresh tomatoes, using a pinch of soda to prevent curdling. Now press the contents of the saucepan through a fine sieve, add a heaping teaspoon of butter, reheat, and serve with croutons and 1 tablespoon of whipped cream.

COCKIE-LEEKIE

Put 2 tablespoons of butter in a saucepan, and when melted stir in, a spoonful at a time, 1 cup of pearl barley, taking ten minutes to add it all; then cover with 8 cups of carrot or onion broth (or use water), and add 2 bay leaves, 1 onion with 4 cloves stuck in it, a bouquet of herbs and parsley, 1 stalk of celery, and let simmer for one hour and a half, then strain, reserving some of the barley. Prepare leeks by washing and cutting into 2-inch lengths (using some of the green), and slicing lengthwise, and add them to the soup; put in the barley, and let cook twenty-five minutes and season with salt and pepper.

CREOLE SOUP

Put 1 can of tomatoes, 1 quart of water or vegetable stock, 1 sliced onion, and 1 small sliced carrot, and 1 chopped green pepper together in a saucepan, and let cook for half an hour, then rub through a fine strainer. Return the strained mixture to the double boiler and put in 2 scant tablespoons of boiled rice, 1 teaspoon of salt, ⅛ teaspoon paprika, 1 tablespoon of sugar. Cream 2 tablespoons of butter with 1 tablespoon of flour, and stir into the soup; let boil up once and serve.

HEILBRONN SOUP

Take 3 quarts of water in which vegetables have been boiled (preferably onions or leeks) and let simmer. In another enamelled pan put 1 tablespoon of butter; when melted stir in slowly with a wooden spoon ½ cup of barley, adding a little at a time, until butter is well "taken up." Let it cook for five minutes, stirring constantly, then add (a ladle at a time) 6 or 8 ladles of the hot stock, putting in this amount during ten minutes of stirring. Add ½ the remaining stock, and salt, pepper, and some nutmeg, and let simmer twenty minutes; then the remaining stock and simmer another one-half hour. Peel ¼ pound mushrooms and cut in 4 or 6 pieces each; fry them in butter for five minutes, and add to soup ten minutes before serving and season afresh.

JULIENNE SOUP

Strain any clear vegetable soup, and to each 2 cups of broth add ½ cup of dried "Julienne;" season with salt and pepper and 1 tablespoon of browned butter.

RED LENTIL SOUP

Soak 2 cups of Egyptian lentils in water for eight or ten hours, then drain and shake dry. Put 2 tablespoons of butter in a saucepan and when melted add ⅓ of the lentils and stir well with a flat-ended wooden spoon, letting them cook very slowly; then add another third, and after stirring a few moments, add the remainder. Pour on 6 cups of cooled water in which leeks or onions have boiled, and let simmer for an hour or until the lentils are tender; press through a sieve and return to the fire to reheat. Smooth 1 teaspoon of flour with 1 teaspoon of butter and add to the soup, season with salt and pepper and a dash of nutmeg. Instead of the flour and butter 1 well-beaten egg may be vigorously stirred into the soup after removing it from the fire.

If Egyptian lentils cannot be obtained, canned or dried red kidney beans may be substituted.

CREAM OF LENTIL

Wash 2 cups of Egyptian lentils, then let them soak in 2 quarts of water for twelve hours or more and put them, in this same water, where they will simmer gently over a slow fire. Put 1 tablespoon of butter in a frying pan, and when melted add to it 2 large onions, sliced, 2 carrots and 1 turnip diced, and fry until a delicate brown; add these to the lentils and let cook slowly for about two hours. Press through a sieve, return to the fire, add 2 cups of milk and just before serving, 1 tablespoon of whipped cream, and season with salt and pepper.

HUNGARIAN SOUP

Put 1 cup of German lentils in a saucepan with 2 cups of cold water or vegetable stock, and let boil for an hour. If the water is absorbed before the lentils are tender, add a little more. At the end of the hour pour over them 6 cups of hot water or stock.

Put 1 tablespoon of butter in a frying pan, and when melted add 1 small onion chopped fine and 1 tablespoon of flour and 1 clove of garlic. When browned add this to the soup and at the same time put in ½ cup of diced potatoes. Let simmer gently for half an hour, then press through a sieve, return to the fire, season well with salt and pepper, and add 1 tablespoon of lemon juice or reduced vinegar before serving.

NOODLE OR ALPHABET SOUP

Strain any one of the vegetable soups for stock, add ½ cup of noodles or "alphabets" fifteen minutes before serving.

PURÉE MONGOLE

Put 1 can of tomatoes in a saucepan and with it 2 cups of strong vegetable broth, 1 stalk of celery, 1 slice of onion, 1 bay leaf, 3 allspice, 3 cloves, salt and pepper, and let cook slowly for half an hour. Pour the liquid through a sieve, pressing with it as much of the tomato as will go, reserving the celery. Return to the saucepan, add 1 tablespoon of reduced vinegar, 1 tablespoon of boiled peas, 1 tablespoon of canned string beans, split in half, and the cooked stalk of celery shredded into thin strips two inches long; let simmer for five minutes, season with salt and pepper, add 1 tablespoon of butter, remove from the fire, and beat vigorously into the soup 1 well-beaten egg.

MUSHROOM BISQUE

Cut up with a silvered knife about 1 cup of fresh mushrooms, wash and drain, toss about in 2 tablespoons of melted butter for ten minutes, then stir in 1 tablespoon of flour made smooth in a little milk, and add 1 quart of milk and let simmer half an hour. Season with salt and paprika, and press through a sieve, reserving half the mushrooms. Add these to the soup, and serve with croutons.

MUSHROOM STEW

Select mushrooms that are white and firm and small, wash them carefully one at a time with the hands, and put 1 heaping cup of them into 4 cups of milk and let heat, without boiling, for 15 minutes. Then add 1 tablespoon of butter, plenty of salt and pepper, and serve in a hot tureen with crisp crackers.

MUSHROOM SOUP

Take ¼ of a pound of fresh mushrooms, ¾ of a cup of small white beans, the rind of half a lemon, 1 Spanish onion in which 5 cloves have been stuck, a small piece of mace, some parsley and thyme, and, after preparing for cooking, let boil for an hour or more in 2 quarts of water; then press all but a few of the mushrooms through a wire strainer, return to the saucepan, add 2 tablespoons of butter, pepper, and salt, ½ teaspoon of soup browning, and, after cutting them in several pieces, add reserved mushrooms and serve.

CREAM OF ONION SOUP

Chop enough onions to make 4 cups, and put them in a large saucepan with 2 tablespoons of butter and stir them for five minutes; then add 1 small onion with 4 cloves stuck in it, a sprig of parsley, and a bay leaf, cover with 6 or 7 cups of water, add salt and pepper, and let cook gently for three quarters of an hour. Press all through a sieve, and return the liquid to the saucepan; add 1 tablespoon of flour blended with 1 tablespoon of butter, also 2 cups of milk (or half cream), and let boil up once before serving. One tablespoon of chopped chives may be added, also 1 tablespoon of whipped cream.

PRINCESS SOUP

Slice 3 onions and cook in a scant half cup of butter for ten minutes. Add 1 quart of hot milk and cook slowly another ten minutes. Strain into double boiler, thicken with 1 teaspoon of flour dissolved in a little milk, and just before serving add 2 teaspoons of finely chopped canned pimentos, and salt and pepper. Add 1 tablespoon of cream in serving.

OKRA SOUP

Cut into small pieces 2 cups (1 can) of okra, use 1 can of green peas, 1 of green corn, 1 cup of shell beans, 2 onions, 1 slice of carrot, 1 slice of turnip, 2 tomatoes, and some celery, or use celery salt. Put 2 tablespoons of butter in a frying pan, and when melted add the chopped onion, carrot, and turnip, and cook ten minutes; then put with the okra, celery and beans into 4 cups of water. Cook for one hour, then add salt and pepper and the tomatoes, corn, peas, and celery, and simmer for half an hour. Do not strain to serve, but if too thick, thin with stock or water.

ONION SOUP AU FROMAGE

Slice 6 ordinary onions or 3 large Spanish ones, and put in frying pan with 2 heaping tablespoons of butter, and let fry *very* slowly until the onions are a rich dark brown,—about fifteen minutes; then scrape the contents of the pan into a large marmite, add 1 large tablespoon of butter, some pepper and salt, and nearly fill the casserole with tepid water, or with water in which onions have boiled; cover and let cook slowly half an hour, and then stir in 2 teaspoons of soup browning. Take 4 thick slices of dry rye bread, spread them thickly with grated cheese, and lay these in the soup pot; remove the cover and let cook five minutes more, and serve in the marmite.

NEW GREEN PEA SOUP

Shell half a peck of peas and wash the pods. Put the pods in a large kettle and almost cover with boiling water; let them simmer for half an hour, then strain these out, and put the peas in this water to boil until tender. The length of time this takes depends on the freshness of the peas. Save out 1 cup of the peas and press the remainder, water and all, through a sieve, and add to them 1 pint of milk, then return to the fire. Rub together 1 tablespoon of flour and one of butter and stir into the boiling soup; then add the reserved cup of peas, season with salt and pepper, and serve. If the flavour of mint is liked, put 3 or 4 mint leaves, or 1 teaspoon of chopped mint, into the tureen. If mint is not used add a little chopped parsley.

CREAM OF GREEN PEA SOUP

Put 1 can of peas, 1 chopped onion, and 1 cup of water in a saucepan, and cook twenty minutes. At the same time put 1 quart of milk on the fire in a double boiler. When the milk is hot stir in 1 tablespoon of butter, and as it boils, 1 tablespoon of flour which has been dissolved in a quarter of a cup of milk. Rub the peas through a fine sieve, stir into the milk, season with salt and pepper, add 1 teaspoon of chopped parsley, and serve. Instead of the parsley, chopped mint can be used if the flavour is liked, or 1 or 2 mint leaves laid in the tureen before the soup is poured in give a delicate flavour.

SPLIT GREEN PEA SOUP

Soak 2 cups of peas for twelve hours or more, and then drain and toss them for ten minutes in a saucepan with 1 tablespoon of butter and 1 tablespoon of chopped onion; then add 4 cups of hot water and let cook two hours, and press through a sieve with the water in which they cooked. Add 1 cup of milk and 1 teaspoon of chopped mint (fresh or dried), and 1 tablespoon whipped cream. Season well with salt and pepper.

POTATO SOUP

Wash 6 to 9 potatoes and put them in boiling water and boil them from twenty minutes to half an hour, the time depending on their size. Use 1 large onion quartered, with cloves stuck in it, and 2 pieces of celery (or ¼ teaspoon of celery salt or celery seed), some mace, 1 bay leaf, and 6 peppercorns, and put in a double boiler with 1 quart of milk, from which reserve 1 small half cup. Mix 1 tablespoon of flour with the reserved milk, and stir slowly into the milk when it boils, and let cook ten minutes longer. When the potatoes are done pour off the water, peel them and mash until light, then add to the boiling milk, stir well, season with salt and pepper, and rub all through a sieve. Return to double boiler, add 1 tablespoon of butter, 1 teaspoon of minced parsley, boil up once, and serve.

POTATO SOUP FLORA

Put 1 tablespoon of butter in a saucepan, and when melted add 1 large onion chopped fine, stir until browned, then add 3 cups of thinly sliced potatoes and 6 cups of cold water; when the potatoes are cooked to a mush press them through a sieve, add a small piece of butter, pepper, and salt, and 1 teaspoon finely chopped parsley.

GERMAN POTATO SOUP

The German potato soup is made by rubbing 6 or 8 well-boiled potatoes through a sieve together with enough of the water in which they were cooked to make sufficient soup, and adding 1 tablespoon of chopped chives (or shallot or onion), 1 teaspoon of chopped parsley, ½ cup of sour cream containing a little lemon juice, or, instead of sour cream, 1 tablespoon of reduced vinegar can be used, with ½ cup of fresh cream. Let simmer for fifteen minutes and serve very hot with croutons.

CREAM OF RICE SOUP

Put ½ cup of rice into 1½ pints of boiling water, and add 2 onions into which 4 cloves are pressed, a piece of celery (or ¼ teaspoon celery seed), one bay leaf, 1 sprig of parsley, 4 peppercorns, and a bit of mace. Let simmer gently for one hour, then turn the soup into a large bowl, pouring it through a fine sieve, and pressing as much through the sieve as possible. Return the contents of the bowl to the saucepan and add 1 pint of milk, 1 teaspoon of salt, 1 tablespoon of butter, and 1 scant tablespoon of flour dissolved in a little milk. Add 1 tablespoon of chopped Spanish pimentos, 1 teaspoon finely chopped chives, let simmer five minutes, add 1 tablespoon of whipped cream, and serve.

RICE AND TOMATO SOUP

Boil 1 cup of rice in 2 quarts of water. Heat the contents of 1 can of tomatoes with 1 bay leaf, 2 slices of onion, and, after fifteen minutes' cooking, press through a sieve and put in double boiler, and to this add 1 pint of water in which rice has been boiled. When hot put in 1 teaspoon of butter, some pepper, salt, and a dash of celery salt, and 2 tablespoons of the cooked rice, and serve. The boiled rice can be utilised for the same meal, or used later.

RICE-OKRA SOUP

Put 2 tablespoons of butter in a large saucepan, and when melted add 1 sliced onion and let simmer for five minutes; then stir in 1 tablespoon of flour, and when smooth and browned add 6 cups of water; season well and let cook slowly for three quarters of an hour. In another saucepan put ¼ cup of rice and 2 cups of sliced okra, and strain the hot stock over the rice and okra, season well with salt and pepper, cover closely, and let simmer gently for an hour. If fresh okra is not available the canned okra is a very good substitute; but if it is used, do not add it to the rice and stock until twenty minutes before removing the soup from the fire.

OYSTER PLANT (SALSIFY) SOUP

Use enough salsify to make 4 cups when sliced. Soak in cold water for an hour, then scrape and put in fresh water, containing some lemon juice, for fifteen minutes. The salsify must not be left out of the water, or it will turn dark. Cut in thin slices, and put into a saucepan containing 4 cups of water and ½ cup of milk, and let cook slowly for about an hour, adding 1 teaspoon of salt when it has cooked half the time. Reserve ¼ of a cup of the salsify, and press the remainder, with the stock, through a sieve; return to the saucepan, add 1½ cups of milk and 1 cup of cream, and 1 tablespoon of butter rubbed together with 1 tablespoon of flour (or less if a thick soup is not liked), a little salt, a dash of paprika and pepper, and serve very hot with small crackers.

SPINACH-TOMATO SOUP

Put 1 tablespoon of butter into the frying pan, and when melted add 1 onion chopped fine, and let cook slowly for ten minutes. Put 1 cup of cold prepared spinach into the butter and onion and 1 cup of tomato sauce or tomatoes, and let heat through. Put 2 cups of milk in a double boiler with 1 tablespoon of flour and 1 of butter rubbed together. Add a pinch of soda to the tomato-spinach mixture, press it through a sieve, and stir the purée into the milk when it boils. Season with salt and pepper and add 1 tablespoon of cream.

CREAM OF SPINACH

Put the contents of 1 can of spinach in a chopping-bowl and chop it to a fine pulp; then put it in a double boiler with 2 tablespoons of onion juice (grated onion), and some salt and pepper, and 5 or 6 cups of milk. Let all cook together for twenty minutes, then pour through a sieve, pressing the spinach to extract the juice. Return the soup to the double boiler, add 1 tablespoon of butter, re-season with salt and pepper and a pinch of nutmeg or mace, and some celery salt. A tablespoon of whipped cream added at the last is an improvement, or 1 tablespoon of finely chopped white and riced yolk of hard-boiled egg can be added. The spinach itself can be prepared next day in any of the ways described for serving spinach.

GERMAN SORREL SOUP

The Germans enrich the above soup by pouring it upon a ½ cup of milk in which the yolks of 2 eggs have been beaten. Do not reverse the process, as it will curdle the soup.

FRENCH SORREL SOUP

Wash 1 quart of sorrel and put it to cook in cold water, remove from the fire in ten minutes and drain and chop fine. Put 2 tablespoons of butter in a saucepan and fry in it when melted 1 small onion chopped fine; then add the sorrel to this and stir for three or four minutes and add 2 cups of cold milk and let simmer for five minutes. Dissolve in 1 cup of milk, 1 teaspoon of sugar and 1 tablespoon of potato flour (or other thickening), and add to the boiling soup; then strain, reheat, and serve with the addition of 1 tablespoon of whipped cream.

ST. GERMAIN SOUP

Take 2 cans of peas, reserving ½ cup of them, and put them in a double boiler with 1 onion cut in 4 pieces with a clove stuck in each, 1 tablespoon of salt, 1 saltspoon of pepper, 1 teaspoon of sugar, 1 bay leaf, and a sprig of parsley; cover and let cook for half an hour, then mash the contents of the double boiler with a potato-masher, and add to them 6 cups of water, and when this boils add to the soup 2 tablespoons of butter and 2 of flour rubbed together; stir well and cook fifteen minutes, then press through a sieve. Return to the double boiler, add 2 cups of milk, the ½ cup of peas drained dry, and reheat, seasoning afresh before serving with croutons.

SPAGHETTI SOUP

Melt 1 tablespoon of butter in a large saucepan, and add to it 1 thinly sliced onion, 2 slices of carrot, 2 slices of turnip, ½ cup of chopped celery (or 1 teaspoon of celery seed may be used instead), and let cook very slowly. Stir frequently, and at the end of ten minutes add 2 cloves, 10 or 12 peppercorns, a small piece of cinnamon, and 1 large bay leaf, and 8 cups (or 2 quarts) of cold water. Cover the saucepan and let the soup cook slowly three quarters of an hour, then strain carefully and return to the saucepan. Season with 1 teaspoon of salt, and add ½ cup of spaghetti broken into inch-long pieces. Cover the saucepan and let the soup *simmer* for an hour, as this will draw more flavour from the spaghetti than rapid boiling, and is the better way for a soup, since the object is to extract the flavour of the ingredients. Grated or Parmesan cheese served with this soup is an improvement.

SCOTCH BROTH

Put 2 quarts of water in kettle, and when at boiling point add ½ cup of pearl barley, which has been tossed in hot butter in a frying pan for five minutes, and let cook slowly. Cut up 2 carrots, 2 turnips, and 3 large onions, and fry in 2 tablespoons of butter. Chop a sprig of parsley very fine, and put with the other vegetables into the barley and water. Let cook slowly for two hours, season with pepper and salt, and serve. A ½ teaspoon of soup-browning improves the appearance of the broth.

SPANISH TOMATO SOUP

Put 1 tablespoon of butter in a saucepan, and when melted stir into it 3 onions thinly sliced, and let simmer for ten minutes; then add to them the juice from 1 can of tomatoes and 2 of the tomatoes, and let cook slowly for twenty minutes; strain, pressing through a sieve, return to the fire, add 1 tablespoon of butter, some pepper and salt, and stir in 2 well-beaten eggs. Do not let the soup boil after adding the eggs.

TOMATO-TAPIOCA SOUP

Put 2 quarts of water into a double boiler, and when it boils add ½ cup of tapioca. Slice 6 large tomatoes (or use 2 cups of strained canned tomatoes), cut 2 onions fine, and fry together until a light brown in 1 tablespoon of butter. Scrape the contents of the pan into the kettle and let simmer slowly for an hour and a half, then season well and serve.

TOMATO CREAM SOUP

Take 2 cups of canned tomatoes, juice and all, mash the large pieces to a pulp, and place in a saucepan with 1½ cups of hot water and a piece of butter the size of an egg, a pinch of pepper, ½ teaspoon of salt, and 1 bay leaf. Let come to a boil, and then add ¼ teaspoon of carbonate of soda, stir for one minute, and add 2 cups of milk. Let boil up and pour in tureen in which is a ½ cup of cracker crumbs very finely rolled. Use this way for ordinary use, or strain to serve in cups.

TOMATO AND CORN BISQUE

Put 1 quart of milk and 1 can of corn in a double boiler and let simmer fifteen minutes; then add 1 teaspoon of butter, season well with salt and pepper, and press through a sieve, and put back into the double boiler. Add ½ cup of boiled tomatoes which have been pressed through a sieve, stir together, reheat, and serve.

TOMATO-MACARONI SOUP

Put 1 can of tomatoes, 1 sprig of parsley, 1 onion with 4 cloves stuck in it, 1 tablespoon of salt, 6 peppercorns, and 6 cups of cold water in a saucepan, and let cook slowly for three quarters of an hour; then strain and return to the saucepan, and when boiling again, add ½ cup of macaroni which has been broken into small pieces, and cover and cook for half an hour. Season afresh before serving. Spaghetti or noodles may be used instead of macaroni.

TOMATO SOUP

Let 1 quart can of tomatoes, 2 cups of water (or rice stock), a sprig of parsley, 1 bay leaf, and 1 onion simmer together for fifteen minutes, then press through a sieve and return to the fire to boil. Rub 1 tablespoon of butter and 1 tablespoon of flour together, and stir into the boiling soup until smooth. Add salt, pepper, and a pinch of soda, and serve immediately with croutons. If water in which rice has boiled is used omit the flour and the soda.

TOMATO-OKRA SOUP

Into 1½ quarts (6 cups) of boiling water put ½ cup of rice; cover and let boil fifteen minutes, then add the contents of 1 can of "tomato-okra" and cook ten minutes more. Reserve 2 okra pods, 2 tomatoes, and 1 tablespoon of rice, and press all the rest through a sieve. Return to the fire, season with salt and pepper, and add the rice and tomatoes and the okra cut in thin slices.

VEGETABLE SOUP. NO. 1

Cut in tiny squares 1 potato, 1 onion, ½ turnip, 1 carrot, and 1 root of celery. Melt 1 tablespoon of butter in a frying pan, add all vegetables except the potato, and fry until a delicate brown. Scrape the contents of the frying pan into a kettle containing 2 quarts of cold water, 1 teaspoon of salt, 3 tablespoons of rice, 1 bay leaf, and a bunch of soup herbs. Cook slowly for one hour and a half, and then add the potatoes and boil twenty minutes more. Add pepper, a little fresh salt, and 1 teaspoon soup-browning, and, if a thin soup is preferred, strain out most of the vegetables and rice. These may be served with brown sauce and put in individual crust cups made hot in oven after being filled.

VEGETABLE SOUP. NO. 2

When seasonable another vegetable soup may be made, proceeding as above, but adding cauliflower and young onions instead of carrots, etc., and thinning with 1½ cups of hot milk and adding at the last ½ cup of boiled young peas. Add butter, pepper, and salt, and a spoonful of cream, before serving.

VEGETABLE SOUP. NO. 3

Put 1 generous tablespoon of butter in a large saucepan, and fry in the butter when melted ½ cup of chopped onion, and when a golden brown stir in carefully 1 tablespoon of flour, and when smoothed pour on slowly 2 cups of hot water or vegetable stock. Now put in ½ cup each of chopped carrot, turnip, parsnip, and 1 cup of celery, and dredge well with pepper and salt, and cover with boiling water, and let simmer for one hour. Then put in 2 cups of parboiled potatoes, and when the vegetables are soft press through a sieve with the stock in which they have cooked.

VEGETABLE SOUP. NO. 4

A much more simple but very palatable vegetable soup is made by taking 1 cup of diced carrots and 1 cup of parsnips and 1 can of peas (or fewer peas can be used), covering them with cold water, and after one hour's boiling adding 2 cups of milk, to which should be added when it boils 1 teaspoon of potato-flour, or other thickening, and, before serving, pepper, salt, and a small piece of butter.

VEGETABLE SOUP. NO. 5

Slice and cut in fancy shapes 1 turnip, 1 carrot, 1 sweet potato, the corn from 1 ear of corn, or use 2 tablespoons of canned corn, and strain ½ can of peas, or ½ cup of fresh peas may be used. Put 3 quarts of water in a saucepan, and when boiling add 1 tablespoon of rice and the carrot; let boil for half an hour, then put in the other vegetables and cook for half an hour longer, and add 1 tablespoon of chopped parsley before serving; also season highly with salt and pepper.

CREAM OF VEGETABLE SOUP

Melt 3 tablespoons of butter in a saucepan, and add 3 tablespoons each of chopped celery, turnip, and carrot, and 1 tablespoon of minced onion, 4 bay leaves, and 4 blades of mace. Cook together very slowly for twenty minutes, stirring frequently to prevent browning; then shake in 3 tablespoons of flour, and when blended put the contents of the frying pan into a little less than 3 pints of milk made hot in a double boiler. Cook twenty minutes longer, and then season well with salt and pepper, and pour into a saucepan containing 2 egg-yolks, beaten with ½ cup of cream or milk. The soup can then be strained and served without any, or with only a few, of the vegetables, or it is delicious served without straining. It can be made at any time that is convenient and reheated for serving.

MULLIGATAWNY SOUP

Make as above, but strain, reserving a little rice and a little tomato to add later; stir 1 tablespoon of curry paste (or powder) into the soup, reheat, and serve.

PURÉE OF VEGETABLE MARROW
(SUMMER SQUASH)

Slice 3 onions and cover with 2 quarts of cold water, and when it boils add a large vegetable marrow, cut in thin slices. Let simmer slowly for two hours, then rub all through a sieve; mix 1 tablespoon of ground rice, 1 cup of milk, and 1 tablespoon of butter in a saucepan, and when hot add to the soup. Finish with 2 tablespoons of boiled flageolets, or peas, and season well with salt and pepper.

VEGETABLE DISHES

JERUSALEM ARTICHOKES IN BUTTER

Wash 1 quart of artichokes, scrape them well, and lay them in salted water to keep them from discolouring, then put them in salted, boiling water which has been whitened with a little milk, and boil for twenty or twenty-five minutes. Drain and arrange in a buttered baking dish; pour over them 3 tablespoons of melted butter, and sprinkle the tops with browned bread crumbs finely rolled, and set them in the oven for five minutes.

This dish makes a dainty entremets when served in individual gratin dishes, in which case 2 or 3 artichokes should be arranged in each dish. The little dish should be served on a small plate with a paper doiley.

JERUSALEM ARTICHOKES AU GRATIN

Prepare the artichokes as in above recipe, arrange them in a large baking dish, or in small individual dishes, cover them with white sauce, sprinkle the top with grated cheese and crumbs, and put them in the oven a few minutes to brown.

JERUSALEM ARTICHOKES WITH TOMATO SAUCE

Prepare the artichokes as in the first recipe, but instead of using melted butter use a little tomato sauce, and sprinkle the artichokes with browned crumbs, and let heat a few moments in the oven before serving. This also is a dainty dish to serve after the soup in individual gratin dishes.

JERUSALEM ARTICHOKES WITH FRENCH SAUCE

Prepare as directed, and in the water in which the artichokes are boiling put 1 large onion and a piece of celery finely chopped. After removing the artichokes take enough of the stock for a sauce, season it nicely, thicken with the yolk of an egg, and strain and pour over the hot artichokes and serve.

JERUSALEM ARTICHOKE FRITTERS

Boil the artichokes not more than fifteen minutes, cut them into strips ¼ of an inch thick, dry them, dip them in flour, and then in batter, and fry a golden brown in good butter.

FRIED ARTICHOKES

Boil as directed, but do not quite finish cooking; let them cool, slice them and fry in melted butter, adding 1 teaspoon of chopped parsley just before removing from the pan.

FRENCH FRIED JERUSALEM ARTICHOKES

Scrape and wash 1 quart of Jerusalem artichokes, cut in slices lengthwise, and fry in a frying basket in hot vegetable fat or oil until a golden brown. Serve with a sprinkling of lemon juice, or with Dutch butter and browned crumbs.

JERUSALEM ARTICHOKES TARTARE

Select small artichokes, or cut them round with a patent cutter, roll them in yolk of egg and then in fine crumbs, place in a frying basket, and fry in hot vegetable fat until a golden brown. Serve very hot, garnished with parsley, and with a tureen of sauce Tartare. Serve alone after soup.

FRIED ARTICHOKES WITH TOMATO SAUCE

Fry artichokes as in foregoing recipe and serve with hot tomato sauce.

JERUSALEM ARTICHOKES LYONNAISE

Boil the artichokes as directed, but do net let them quite finish cooking, then slice them. Put 1 tablespoon of butter in a frying pan, and when melted add 1 large onion sliced or chopped, and when onions are transparent, but not brown, add the artichokes and fry slowly. Sprinkle with chopped parsley or chives.

JERUSALEM ARTICHOKE PURÉE

Boil 1 quart of artichokes as already directed, drain, mash and press through a fine sieve, and stir in 2 tablespoons of melted butter; then stir over a low fire until the moisture is exhausted. Remove from the fire, and when cold add 4 eggs which have been well beaten, beating them briskly, and adding them slowly to the purée; also beat in 1 tablespoon of whipped cream. When thoroughly mixed and light from much beating put into a large mould, or into individual moulds, and steam or poach with water half-way up the mould, and turn out and serve with some good sauce, tomato or Hollandaise preferred, or the sauce described as being made with the water in which the artichokes were boiled can be used; to it should be added 1 teaspoon of finely chopped parsley.

JERUSALEM ARTICHOKES NEWBURG

Make a sauce with 2 cups of milk, 1 tablespoon of butter mixed with 1 of flour, 2 yolks of eggs, and pepper and salt, and when thickened add 2 tablespoons of sherry, and 3 cups of sliced boiled artichokes, and ½ cup of blanched chopped almonds. Serve on toast or in cases.

GLOBE ARTICHOKES VINAIGRETTE

Serve cold boiled artichokes, which have been cut in half and the "thistles" removed, with sauce vinaigrette, which is French dressing to which a little chopped onion or onion juice and chopped parsley have been added.

FRENCH OR GLOBE ARTICHOKES

The globe artichoke is a most delicious addition to a vegetarian menu, and it is not because it is not known to be edible, but because many people do not know how either to eat it or to serve it, that it is not oftener seen in America. I have had it served to me in almost every European country and often in restaurants in America, and have never encountered but one cook who knew how it should be sent to the table after cooking, and one waiter who knew how to serve it when it got there. It is usually served half cold with the leaves falling all about it because the "thistle," and usually the best of the artichoke besides, has been carelessly removed in the kitchen; instead of which it should be served whole, as in this way only can it be kept hot enough to be palatable. The artichoke should be set stem end downward on a hot, flat dish and wound about at the base with a small table napkin, and the person who serves it, holding it in the napkin, should reverse it and taking a small, sharp, silvered knife should cut through the artichoke on the bottom, using a sawing motion, and with the help of a serving fork ease apart the "thistle" and the closely knitted small leaves in the centre. Unless the artichokes are very large ones, a half of one is not too much to serve each person. The "thistle" should be removed by the server, and this should be done by carefully separating it from the "fond" or base, which is the fleshy part from which the leaves grow out. The leaves should be taken one by one, by the dry tip, in the fingers, and the fleshy end thus pulled from the base should be dipped in the sauce served, and the soft portion removed by drawing it between the front teeth; when the leaves are finished the base should be cut up with a fork and eaten with the sauce.

FONDS D'ARTICHAUT

The bottom or solid part of the globe artichoke can be bought preserved in bottles; heat them in their own liquid, drain, and serve hot with Hollandaise sauce, or cold with sauce vinaigrette or mayonnaise.

TO STEAM GLOBE ARTICHOKES

Prepare for cooking as in the above recipe, place in a covered steamer, and let steam forty minutes or until the leaves, when pulled, part easily from the base.

TO BOIL GLOBE ARTICHOKES

Globe artichokes should not look dry and wrinkled when bought, but green and fresh. Put them in cold salted water and a little vinegar for fifteen minutes to cleanse and free from insects, then put them in salted boiling water and boil until the leaves part easily from the base when pulled; this should be in about half an hour, but the time varies with the age and size of the artichoke; it should then be drained and the stem cut off so that it will stand erect on the serving dish.

GLOBE ARTICHOKES STUFFED WITH MUSHROOMS

Cut the stalk from fresh artichokes and trim the leaves to an even length, and boil them for twenty minutes, or until the choke or thistle can be removed neatly. Put 1 tablespoon of butter in a frying pan, and when melted add 2 finely minced shallots (or use chives or onion tops), and 1 teaspoon of chopped parsley, and 1 cup of chopped fresh or canned mushrooms, salt and pepper, and fry all together for five minutes. Fill the artichoke with this, tie the leaves together and set in a pan containing 1 cup of stock (or water), 2 tablespoons of butter or olive oil, and bake them half an hour, basting them thoroughly five or six times. Remove the strings, set upright and serve very hot with Dutch butter, or any sauce preferred.

ASPARAGUS

Asparagus should be carefully looked over and washed, and then tied into a bunch with a piece of tape, with all the heads level, then with a very sharp knife an inch or two of the stalks should be so evenly cut off that the bunch will stand upright. Stand the asparagus in a deep saucepan so that the tips are well out of the water, add 1 teaspoon of salt, put a cover on the saucepan, and let cook about half an hour or twenty-five minutes. In this way the tips are sufficiently steamed by the time the stalks are cooked, and will not be cooked to pieces as when immersed in water.

ASPARAGUS WITH WHITE SAUCE

Having boiled the asparagus as directed, lift it out by plunging a sharp fork into it two or three inches from the bottom, lay it on a hot plate on the top of the stove, cut the tape and arrange 4 or 5 pieces each on long strips of toast, and pour over each 2 tablespoons of nicely seasoned white sauce; arrange neatly on a long platter with the asparagus heads all turned one way.

ASPARAGUS WITH DUTCH BUTTER

Proceed exactly as in above recipe, but instead of the white sauce pour a little melted butter over all, and serve with a small tureen of Dutch butter

HOT ASPARAGUS TIPS

Take a can of asparagus tips, drain and put in a saucepan with 2 tablespoons of melted butter into which some paprika has been shaken. When hot garnish with diamonds of toast to serve, and sprinkle with salt.

WHITE ASPARAGUS

Open canned asparagus at the bottom, and after draining, ease it from the can, so as to prevent the tips from being injured. Lay the stalks evenly in a shallow enamelled pan, cover with hot water or the juice from the can, and let heat through over a slow fire. Remove after ten minutes' cooking to a heated flat dish, using a strainer to lift the stalks from the water. Serve with Dutch butter, into which a few browned crumbs have been stirred, or chopped chives can be used instead of crumbs. The asparagus can also be served with tomato sauce.

ASPARAGUS VINAIGRETTE

Place the can of asparagus to be used on the ice for half an hour, then open and drain and rinse carefully in cold water. Place on crisp lettuce leaves, using 5 or 6 stalks on each, and serve with sauce vinaigrette.

FRIED TIPS WITH ONION BUTTER

Put 1 tablespoon of butter in a saucepan, and when melted add 1 tablespoon of grated onion and the drained contents of 1 can of asparagus tips. Let all cook together slowly for five minutes, and season with salt and pepper.

ASPARAGUS TIPS WITH WHITE SAUCE

Heat 1 can of asparagus tips with 1 tablespoon of melted butter, and to serve, cover with ¾ of a cup of highly seasoned white sauce in which the white of 1 hard-boiled egg has been mixed, after being chopped fine. Sprinkle over the top the yolk of the egg pressed through a sieve, and serve with squares of toast.

ASPARAGUS IN BREAD CASES

Boil 2 cups of asparagus tips in salted water for fifteen minutes, and then drain them; while they are cooking put 1 cup of milk in a double boiler, and when boiling pour some of it on to 2 lightly beaten eggs, stirring vigorously meanwhile, and then put the eggs into the double boiler with the milk, and stir until it begins to thicken. Add 1 teaspoon of butter, ½ teaspoon of salt, and ½ saltspoon of pepper, and remove from the fire. Cut the asparagus tops into half-inch pieces and add them to the sauce. Take 5 stale rolls, cut off the tops, remove the inside, and let them dry in the oven; when crisp and hot fill each with the asparagus in sauce, replace the top and serve.

ESCALLOPED ASPARAGUS

Use either fresh green asparagus, or canned asparagus. Cut it into two-inch lengths, and if fresh is used cook in boiling water for ten minutes. Put 2 tablespoons of butter in a frying pan and brown in it ½ cup of bread crumbs and ½ cup of finely chopped roasted peanuts. Roll each bit of asparagus in beaten egg and the crumbs and nut mixture, and arrange in a buttered gratin dish with alternate layers of thick white sauce, seasoning each layer with a little pepper and salt. Cover the top with crumbs and a sprinkling of grated cheese, and brown in the oven.

GRIDDLED APPLES

Peel and core large sour apples. Cut them in thick slices and lay on a well-buttered griddle, and let fry until a light brown; turn, and brown the other side.

APPLE FRITTERS

Pare and core as many tart apples as required, sprinkle with salt, dip in batter, and fry until golden brown in hot fat. Drain on brown paper before serving.

BOILED BANANAS

Put bananas unpeeled into boiling water, let boil for ten minutes, then peel and cut in two and serve with melted butter.

BANANAS WITH TOMATOES

Peel 3 bananas and cut them in slices either lengthwise or across, and slice 3 or 4 large tomatoes. Put 2 tablespoons of butter in a frying pan, and when melted lay in the bananas and tomatoes and sprinkle well with salt, pepper, and 1 tablespoon of sugar. Let cook slowly, and when browned on the bottom turn and add another sprinkling of sugar, brown again, and serve very hot.

BANANA FRITTERS

Pare the bananas required, cut each in half crosswise, and then split each half. Sprinkle with salt and dip in batter and fry until a golden brown in hot fat. Drain on brown paper and serve very hot.

BOSTON BAKED BEANS

Cover with cold water 3 or 4 cups of dry California pea beans, or any small white beans, and let them soak over night. The next morning drain and put on the stove in a large kettle well filled with water, and let cook slowly, with ¼ of a teaspoon of soda added, for half an hour. Put 2 tablespoons of butter in the bean-pot, or a deep baking dish, drain the beans, and put them in the butter. Pour over them slowly 4 tablespoons of dark molasses, 1 tablespoon of salt, and add 1 tablespoon of butter; then fill the bean-pot to the top with hot water and bake in a very slow oven for 6 or 7 hours. As the water cooks away replace it. This will require doing about three times during the baking. Serve in the dish in which they were cooked, and garnish with whole black pickled walnuts.

GREEN STRING BEANS

If fresh beans are used pick them over, remove the ends and "strings," and boil for half an hour or more; then drain them, and add 1 tablespoon of butter and 2 tablespoons of milk, season with salt and pepper, and serve after ten minutes' slow cooking. If canned beans are used omit the first long boiling.

GOLDEN WAX BEANS

If fresh beans are used wash, remove the ends and "strings," and boil for three quarters of an hour, or until tender, in salted water; then drain and add to them 1 tablespoon of butter, and 2 tablespoons of milk, let cook slowly for ten minutes, and season well with salt and pepper. In using canned beans omit the first boiling.

FRENCH BEANS (FLAGEOLETS)

Those in glass are the best; drain and put in a double boiler with 1 tablespoon of butter, pepper and salt, and 1 tablespoon of cream. Serve very hot.

DRIED BEANS DEUTSCHLAND

Pick over 1½ cups of dried beans of any sort, cover with water, and soak ten hours or more. Drain and put in boiling water (or the stock onions or leeks have boiled in), and let cook slowly for two hours, or until tender but unbroken, then drain. Put 2 tablespoons of butter in a frying pan, and when melted add 1 onion chopped fine, and let it cook slowly for ten minutes; then add the beans and season with salt and pepper and put over them 2 tablespoons of lemon juice or 1 tablespoon of "reduced vinegar," and let cook very slowly for ten or fifteen minutes that all may be well blended before serving.

WHITE BEANS FLORENTINE

Soak 4 cups of white kidney beans for ten hours, then boil them two hours. Slip the skins off and put them into a saucepan with 1 cup of broth and a bunch of sweet herbs, 1 bay leaf, and 2 tablespoons of Marsala or sherry. Cover and let them cook slowly for thirty minutes. Remove the herbs and stir in 1 tablespoon of butter and 1 tablespoon of flour rubbed well together, stir until smooth, and then pour on 1 cup of cream or milk into which 1 egg has been beaten; continue to stir, add 1 tablespoon of lemon juice, 1 tablespoon of chopped parsley, and serve with grated cheese.

BEANS AND CORN ESCALLOPED

Use 1 can of green string beans, or Lima beans, and 1 can of sweet corn. Butter a baking dish, and arrange a layer of beans; dot with butter, and season with pepper and salt, then put on this a layer of corn about half an inch deep, season, and so proceed until the dish is filled. Then pour ½ cup of milk over all, sprinkle with bread crumbs, and bake for fifteen minutes, or until the crumbs are browned.

ITALIAN BEANS

Use 3 cups of white haricot beans, soak for several hours, boil two hours in salted water, then drain. Put 1 tablespoon of butter in a saucepan, and when melted add 1 large onion chopped fine and 2 bay leaves. Let cook slowly for eight minutes, then put into the pan the boiled beans, and season with salt and pepper; let heat through, stirring gently, and add 1 cup of tomato sauce two minutes before removing from the fire.

Canned brown or red beans may be used, giving the same dish practically with far less trouble.

SPANISH BEANS

Soak for eight or ten hours any sort of large dried beans, then drain them and put them into boiling water two hours or more, or until cooked. One way of testing them is to remove a few and blow on them; if the skins crack they are done. Drain, and put them in a bean-pot or casserole and sprinkle with 2 tablespoons of chopped onion and 2 cups of strained tomatoes, and dredge well with salt. Cover the dish and bake slowly for an hour. A quarter of an hour before taking out, pour over them 1 tablespoon of melted butter and remove the cover.

LIMA BEANS

Let Lima beans stand in cold water for an hour or so after they are shelled, and in cooking them allow 8 cups of water to every 4 cups of beans. Put them in boiling salted water, and let them cook for an hour, or more if not fresh picked. Drain them and add ½ cup of the water they cooked in, ½ cup of milk, 1 tablespoon of butter, and season highly with salt and pepper.

Dried beans must soak ten or twelve hours and cook two hours. Canned Lima beans only need reheating, draining, and a little milk and butter and seasoning added to them.

LIMA BEANS HOLLANDAISE

Boil 1 quart of beans until tender, salting them well when half cooked. Beat a large tablespoon of butter to a cream, beat in the yolk of 1 egg, 1 tablespoon of finely chopped parsley, 1 saltspoon of black pepper, and 2 teaspoons of lemon juice; when this sauce is well mixed stir it into the beans, taking care not to break them.

CREAMED LIMA BEANS

Cover 2 cups of boiled Lima beans with 1 scant cup of cream, and let simmer in a double boiler for ten minutes; then add 1 teaspoon of butter, and season with salt, pepper, and a dash of nutmeg.

LIMA BEAN SAUQUETASH

Boil 2 cups of freshly picked Lima beans in 1 quart of water for half an hour, then drain them and add 1 cup of milk, 1 tablespoon of butter, and enough green corn cut from the cob to make 2 cups. Season well, and let simmer for fifteen minutes, and salt again before serving.

If canned corn and canned beans are used they need be cooked for only ten minutes.

BEETS

Great care should be taken in washing beets that the small rootlets are not broken or the skin of the beet bruised, as anything which causes the juice to escape injures both the taste and the colour. In the city, beets are seldom obtainable which require less than two or three hours' cooking; but really young, small beets should not require more than one hour's boiling. When boiled they should be drained, then plunged into cold water, after which the skin can be rubbed off with the hand. Some, however, prefer that beets should be baked or steamed; the time required to cook will then be somewhat longer. Canned beets are a great convenience.

CREAMED BEETS

Boil 6 or 7 medium-sized beets until tender, then remove them from the saucepan and place them in cold water; rub the skins off carefully with the hands, and cut them in half-inch cubes. Make a sauce of 2 tablespoons of butter creamed with 2 tablespoons of flour and ½ cup of the water in which the beets were boiled, 2 tablespoons of cream, 2 tablespoons of vinegar, 2 teaspoons of sugar, ½ teaspoon of salt, and 1 saltspoon of pepper. Pour the sauce over the hot beets and serve in a heated deep dish.

VIRGINIA BEETS

Carefully peel boiled beets, and with a sharp knife cut into very thin, even slices, laying them as sliced into a heated vegetable dish; when a layer has been made over the bottom, dot it well with butter, season lightly with salt, and sprinkle with 1 tablespoon of granulated sugar; then arrange another layer of beets with butter, salt, and sugar, and proceed in this way until the dish is filled. The work should be done near the fire in order that the beets may not cool, as the dish should be served very hot. If, however, the beets have cooled in preparation, set them in a hot oven for a few minutes, and turn them with a spoon in the dish before serving in order that they may be juicy.

PICQUANT BEETS

Peel hot cooked beets, cut into slices, and toss about for three or four minutes in a saucepan which contains 3 tablespoons of butter to which has been added 1 teaspoon of plain vinegar, or a few drops of tarragon, 2 cloves, and 1 teaspoon of sugar.

GERMAN BEETS

Make a sauce of 1 tablespoon of butter, when melted add 1 tablespoon of flour, 2 teaspoons of onion juice, ½ teaspoon of salt, 1 tablespoon of sugar, 1 tablespoon of lemon juice, and enough hot water to make the sauce the right consistency; then add freshly sliced cooked beets, and let cook together three or four minutes before serving.

PICKLED BEETS

Place slices of cold beets in a deep porcelain or glass receptacle, place some peppercorns among them, and a few allspice, cover with mild vinegar, and let stand ten or twelve hours before using.

BRUSSELS SPROUTS

Brussels sprouts are best if laid for ten minutes, after trimming and looking over, in salted cold water which contains some lemon juice. They should then be drained and put in a large saucepan filled with boiling water containing salt and a pinch of soda. Parboil in this ten minutes, then lift them with a strainer and put in a steamer above the boiling water; cover, and let steam half an hour to finish cooking.

If sprouts are cooked by boiling instead of steaming, leave the saucepan uncovered, as this will keep the odour from being pronounced. Boil in salted water from twenty to thirty minutes, drain the instant they are tender, and serve with melted butter.

BRUSSELS SPROUTS IN DUTCH BUTTER

Put boiled Brussels sprouts in a saucepan with 2 tablespoons of melted butter, to which has been added a tablespoon of lemon juice; stir until hot and add pepper and salt.

BRUSSELS SPROUTS WITH CELERY

Trim and wash in cold running water 1 quart of Brussels sprouts; then place them in a saucepan, cover with boiling water, and let them boil for five minutes; then drain and cover with fresh boiling water containing 1 teaspoon of salt. Boil for another twenty-five minutes *uncovered*, and then drain them. Wash enough celery to make 1½ cups when cut in pieces one inch long, put this in a saucepan with 3 tablespoons of butter, stir well together, and add 1½ cups of scalded milk containing 2 tablespoons of flour; when this is thickened add the sprouts, season with salt and pepper, and serve very hot.

BRUSSELS SPROUTS WITH CHESTNUTS

To every cup of Brussels sprouts allow ½ cup of blanched chestnuts which have been cooked for fifteen minutes; put the sprouts and chestnuts together, cook another forty minutes, drain, and serve with white sauce.

BRUSSELS SPROUTS LYONNAISE

Put 1 tablespoon of butter in a saucepan, and when melted add 1 tablespoon of chopped onion; when this is beginning to brown add 4 cups of boiled sprouts, and stir together for three or four minutes, unless the sprouts were cold, in which case they should be tossed about with the butter and onion until hot.

CREAMED BRUSSELS SPROUTS

Cover freshly boiled Brussels sprouts with a white sauce made entirely of milk, or of the stock in which they were cooked, with 1 tablespoon of cream added.

BRUSSELS SPROUTS IN BREAD CASES

Cut stale bread into three-inch squares, and with a sharp knife cut out the centre, leaving a bottom and four sides like a box; brush over with melted butter, and brown in the oven. Serve sprouts prepared in any of the above ways in these cases; the creamed sprouts are perhaps the best served this way.

CABBAGE

Wash cabbage carefully after cutting it in half, and let it boil for five minutes in well-salted boiling water; pour this water off and re-cover with fresh boiling water; let cook for half an hour, then add 1 teaspoon of salt, and let finish cooking, which will be in about another half an hour for a medium-sized cabbage.

Cabbage should never be covered while boiling, as covering increases the odour in cooking.

NEW ENGLAND CABBAGE

Cut a cabbage in quarters, wash it thoroughly, and parboil it for five minutes in salted water; then drain and cook with 2 carrots and 2 turnips for an hour or until tender, in any strong vegetable stock, to which 1 tablespoon of butter has been added. Drain and dampen with a little of the stock to serve, and season well with salt and pepper.

WESTERN CABBAGE

Take 4 or 5 cups of shredded white cabbage and put in a frying pan in which 1 tablespoon of butter has been melted. Press the cabbage into the pan, dredge with salt and pepper, and pour over it ½ cup of vinegar and ½ cup of water; cover and let cook very gently for half an hour or somewhat less.

Red cabbage can be prepared in this same way, and a pretty dish is made by using equal quantities of red and white cabbage.

CABBAGE SARMAS

Put 1 tablespoon of butter in a saucepan, and when melted add 1 onion chopped fine, and after it has cooked gently for ten minutes stir into it 1 cup of boiled rice, ½ cup of chopped nuts, 1 teaspoon of salt, 1 saltspoon of pepper, and 1 tablespoon of melted butter. Parboil a small cabbage for fifteen minutes, then separate its leaves, and into each leaf roll 1 tablespoon of the force-meat; pack tightly in a shallow pan, dredge with salt and pepper, and cover with the water in which the cabbage cooked; lay 2 bay leaves on the top, and let simmer for fifteen minutes. Serve with melted butter or tomato sauce.

CABBAGE LICHTENSTEIN

Cut one large cabbage into small pieces, not using the stalk. Wash well and put in a kettle of boiling water with 1 teaspoon of salt and 1 tablespoon of caraway seed. Cook for half an hour uncovered, then add to the cabbage 4 large potatoes peeled and quartered, season afresh with salt, and let cook another twenty minutes. Put 2 tablespoons of butter in a frying pan, and when melted add 1 onion chopped fine and 1 tablespoon of flour; let all cook together until brown, then scrape the contents of the frying pan into the cabbage, etc., and cook slowly for twenty minutes more, or until the stock is almost cooked away.

LADY CABBAGE

Boil firm white cabbage fifteen minutes, changing the water then for more from the boiling teakettle; continue boiling for half an hour or until tender, then drain and set aside until perfectly cold. Chop fine, season with pepper and salt, add 1 or 2 well-beaten eggs, 1 tablespoon of butter, and ½ cup of rich milk. Stir all well together and bake in a buttered dish until brown. The oven should be moderately hot, and the same care used as in the baking of a custard. Serve in the baking dish.

COLD SLAW

Put 2 tablespoons of vinegar on to boil in a saucepan, and add to it when boiling ½ cup of sour or fresh milk or cream containing 2 lightly beaten eggs; stir and then add 1 tablespoon of butter, salt and pepper, and pour over 4 cups of shredded cabbage arranged in a deep bowl. Serve cold.

GERMAN RED CABBAGE

Put 3 or 4 cups of shredded red cabbage into a saucepan with 1 tablespoon of butter, 1 finely chopped apple, and the juice of half a lemon; sprinkle lightly with sugar, season with salt and pepper, cover, and let cook from half to three quarters of an hour.

HUNGARIAN CABBAGE

Quarter a red cabbage, remove the stalk parts and wash well, and put it in a kettle containing enough boiling water to cover it. Let boil for three quarters of an hour or until tender, and then drain, gently pressing out all the water. Put 2 tablespoons of butter in a frying pan, and when melted add 1 onion chopped fine and 1 tablespoon of flour; stir until smooth and let cook until brown. Then add ½ cup of brown sugar, ⅓ of a cup of vinegar, and salt well. Add the shredded cabbage to this, and let all simmer together for fifteen or twenty minutes before serving.

PICKLED RED CABBAGE

Chop or shred enough cabbage to make 2 quarts (8 cups) and add to it 1 large onion chopped fine and 1 tablespoon of salt; mix well together and let stand over night in a covered jar. Next day press through a colander to drain, and then place a layer of cabbage in a jar, sprinkle over it a few mustard seeds and 2 or 3 cloves, and proceed in this way until the cabbage is all used. Do not press down. Cover with cider vinegar, and use any time after twenty-four hours.

CREAMED CARROTS

Scrape and wash enough carrots to make 4 cups when cut in dice, and put them in a double boiler containing half milk and half water at boiling point. Let them cook slowly for forty minutes or until tender, then drain them and put them in a hot dish at the side of the stove. Use 1 cup of the stock they cooked in to make a sauce, with 1 tablespoon of butter, 1 of flour, and plenty of salt and pepper. Pour the sauce over them to serve.

CREAMED CARROTS AND POTATOES

To 1 quart of cold boiled potatoes, cut in dice, add 1 cup of boiled diced carrots. Put them in a double boiler and cover with 1½ cups of highly seasoned white sauce, to which has been added 1 tablespoon of onion juice and 1 tablespoon of finely chopped parsley; let boil up once and serve.

CARROTS SAUTÉ

Use boiled carrots cut in dice or fancy shapes and toss them for five minutes in hot butter. Season with salt and pepper, add a little chopped parsley, and serve very hot. Fancy shaped German carrots in glass bottles can be used instead of fresh ones.

GLORIFIED CARROTS

Take 2 cups of diced carrots and boil them in slightly sweetened water about half an hour, or until tender, and let them cool. Put 1 tablespoon of butter into a saucepan, add to it 1 teaspoon of grated onion, and toss together until hot; then add the diced carrots and 1 cup of well-made white sauce. Butter small individual gratin dishes, fill them with the carrot mixture, sprinkle the top with a few lightly browned bread crumbs, then with chopped chives, and set in a hot oven for five minutes. Serve alone as an entrée, placing each dish on a small plate with a paper doily.

This dish can be varied by using more chives mixed with the carrots and omitting the onion, or, if chives are not at hand, they can be omitted when the onion is used, and finely chopped parsley substituted to garnish the top.

The quantities given here can be doubled, and the carrots cooked in a large baking dish as an addition to the main course of a luncheon or dinner.

GLAZED CARROTS

For this, the carrots must be cut into even cones or ovals, and it is convenient to use the imported carrots in glass bottles. If these are used they are already boiled; if fresh carrots are used scrape and wash them and cut out the little shapes with a patent cutter, then boil slowly until tender, but not quite done, and put 2 or 3 cups of them in a frying pan with 2 tablespoons of butter, which has been melted, sprinkle with fine sugar, and stir over a hot fire until they begin to brown; then add 2 tablespoons of the stock they boiled in, continue to stir them, add more stock if needed, and continue stirring until the carrots are nicely glazed. Serve alone or as a garnish.

CARROTS DELMONICO

Scrape and cut in dice enough carrots to fill a small baking dish; cover with boiling water in which is 1 tablespoon of sugar, and 1 tablespoon of butter, and let cook for half an hour, or until tender. Drain and let them cool, and then arrange them in the baking dish with the following sauce: Melt 3 tablespoons of butter, add 3 tablespoons of flour, and when this is smooth stir into it, using a little at a time, 1 cup of the stock in which the carrots were cooked, ½ cup of cream or milk containing the beaten yolks of 2 eggs; when smooth add ½ tablespoon of lemon juice, and salt and pepper well. Sprinkle the top with finely rolled crumbs and let brown in the oven.

CARROT SOUFFLÉ

Mix 2 cups of boiled, mashed carrots, 2 tablespoons of chopped onion, fried for five minutes in 1 tablespoon of butter, 1 cup of milk or cream in which 3 egg-yolks are beaten, ½ teaspoon of nutmeg, salt and pepper, and when well blended add lightly with a fork the stiffly beaten whites of the 3 eggs. Sprinkle with bread crumbs and bake to brown about fifteen or twenty minutes.

CAULIFLOWER

Leave all the green that looks fresh and palatable on the cauliflower, and wash it and let it stand from fifteen minutes to half an hour in salted water. Then put it in a saucepan, stem downwards, with the top barely covered with boiling water, and, if the saucepan is not too large, it will keep the cauliflower upright, so that the delicate top will not cook to pieces before the green stalk is tender. A small cauliflower will take half an hour to cook, and the lower part can be tried with a fork to see when it is tender. Leave the saucepan uncovered in cooking cauliflower, and the odour from the cooking will be very much lessened and the cauliflower more delicate in taste.

CAULIFLOWER AU GRATIN

Boil a large cauliflower, drain it, and break the sprays apart. Arrange in layers in a buttered baking dish, sprinkling each layer with cheese, and seasoning it with pepper and salt. When the dish is filled pour on 1 cup of white sauce, sprinkle the top with crumbs and cheese, and let bake fifteen minutes to brown.

CREAMED CAULIFLOWER

Boil and drain a cauliflower and serve over it 1 cup of white sauce.

CAULIFLOWER IN A GERMAN WAY

Boil a cauliflower and drain it, dredge with salt and pepper, and cover the white part with melted butter, and then dust this with browned bread crumbs; pour ¾ of a cup of Dutch butter over it, and let it heat for five minutes in the oven in the shallow gratin dish in which it should be served.

ITALIAN CAULIFLOWER

Boil and drain a cauliflower and dredge the top with pepper and salt, sprinkle with grated cheese, and pour a little melted butter over it. Set in the oven for five minutes to brown, and serve surrounded with tomato sauce.

CAULIFLOWER FRITTERS

Boil a cauliflower for twenty-five minutes, or until nearly tender, then drain it and let it cool. When cold separate the sprays and dredge with salt and pepper, then dip in batter, and fry in deep fat until a golden brown. Drain and serve very hot.

CREAMED CELERY

Scrape and trim 3 or 4 heads of celery, leaving the roots on and cutting the tops off; cut each stalk in half, lengthwise, and into pieces five inches long; wash carefully in running water, and then blanch in boiling water for ten minutes. Drain and tie the stalks together like bunches of asparagus, and put them in a saucepan containing 2 cups of water, 2 cups of milk, ½ a carrot, ½ an onion with 2 cloves stuck in it, 1 teaspoon of salt, and 1 scant saltspoon of pepper, and let simmer three quarters of an hour or more, or until quite tender when tried with a fork. Remove the celery, strain the stock, and use 1 cup of it in making a sauce, with 1 tablespoon of butter and 1 tablespoon of flour. Untie the bunches of celery, and arrange them evenly on toast with the sauce poured over them.

CELERY IN BROWN SAUCE

Prepare celery as above, boil for three quarters of an hour or until tender, drain, and cover with the brown sauce described below, omitting the wine, and serve in an ordinary vegetable dish.

CELERY IN CASSEROLE

Cut celery in four-inch lengths, halving each stalk lengthwise, and leaving the root on, wash well and parboil for ten minutes in salted water or milk, and arrange in a square, covered casserole. Put 2 tablespoons of butter in a saucepan, and when browned add 2 tablespoons of flour. Stir until well dissolved, then add 2 cups of the water in which the celery cooked, 1 scant teaspoon of salt, 1 small saltspoon of pepper, and 2 bay leaves. Stir until smooth, and then strain and pour this sauce over the celery, add 1 teaspoon of sherry or Madeira, cover the dish, set it in a shallow pan containing a little water, and let it cook for half an hour in the oven. Serve in the casserole.

BAKED CELERY

Cut 2 bunches of celery into two-inch lengths, wash thoroughly, and let blanch in boiling water and milk, using equal quantities of each, for fifteen minutes, then remove the celery and let it cool; add to 1 cup of the milk and water stock 1 tablespoon of butter blended with 1 tablespoon of flour, some pepper and salt, and when smoothed remove from the fire and beat into it vigorously 2 eggs. Arrange the celery in a buttered baking dish, pour the sauce over it, spread the top thickly with crumbs, and put in the oven. Cover for twenty minutes, then uncover and let brown nicely before serving.

CÊPES IN BLACK BUTTER

French Cêpes come in tin or glass. Put 3 tablespoons of butter in a pan, with 2 bay leaves, a few celery seeds and 1 clove of garlic; let it slowly brown. Strain and add cêpes and let them heat in the butter. Season with salt and paprika and serve very hot.

AMERICAN SWEET CORN

Sweet corn on the cob, which has been picked within twenty-four hours of the time of using, should be dropped into rapidly boiling, slightly salted water, and boiled not more than eight or ten minutes.

ROAST CORN

To roast sweet corn, leave the husks on the cob, and put in a slow oven and let bake for half an hour. Take off the husks and silk and serve at once. Some think this method of cooking the delicate American vegetable retains the flavour of the corn more than the usual way of boiling it.

CORN PUDDING

Use 6 or 7 ears of sweet corn, and cut each row down the middle with a sharp knife, and then cut the grains from the ear, and add to them 2 cups of milk, 1 teaspoon of salt, 1 saltspoon of pepper, 1 teaspoon of sugar, 1 tablespoon of melted butter, and 2 slightly beaten eggs. Put this into a baking dish and bake like a custard, in a slow oven for half an hour, taking care it does not cook too long nor get too hot lest it curdle. Canned corn may be used when fresh is out of season.

CORN CREOLE

Put 1 can of corn into a saucepan with 1 tablespoon of chopped green peppers and ½ cup of milk, and cook slowly for ten minutes; then season with salt and pepper and add 1 tablespoon of butter and serve. This may be put in a baking dish, covered with crumbs, and baked for fifteen minutes.

CORN AND TOMATO PIE

Butter a pudding dish and fill it with alternate layers of boiled or canned corn and tomatoes, and season with salt, pepper, and butter; cover the top with pie-crust and bake in a moderately hot oven for fifteen minutes. If a crust is not desired the dish can be covered with bread crumbs and browned. If fresh tomatoes and corn are used the pie will require twice the time to cook, the first half of the time covered with a plate, and the last half uncovered.

CORN PUDDING IN TOMATO OR PEPPER CASES

Bake the preceding in cases made by scooping a large part of the inside from large, solid tomatoes, or in hollowed-out green, sweet peppers.

CORN CHOWDER

Put 1 tablespoon of butter in a saucepan, and when melted add 1 sliced onion, and let cook slowly for five minutes; then add to it 4 cups of potatoes which have been parboiled for five minutes, and then cut in small squares, and 2 cups of boiling water. Let cook for twenty minutes or until the potatoes are tender, then add 1 can of sweet corn, 4 cups of hot milk, 1 tablespoon of butter, and plenty of salt and pepper, and let heat through. Break 8 soda crackers into a deep dish, and pour the chowder over them to serve.

RHODE ISLAND ESCALLOP

Bake 4 medium-sized sweet potatoes for half an hour, then scrape out the potato and chop it into small bits. Boil 2 ears of green corn for ten minutes, run a sharp knife down each row of grains, cutting them in two, and then cut the corn from the cob and mix it with the chopped sweet potato. Butter six individual gratin dishes and fill them with the mixed corn and potato, sprinkle them with salt, pour 1 tablespoon of melted butter over each, cover with bread crumbs, and let cook for eight or ten minutes in the oven. The same mixture can be used to fill a baking dish, and enough melted butter used to moisten the potato thoroughly.

STEWED CUCUMBERS

Peel 4 or 5 cucumbers, quarter them, and cover them with boiling salted water, and let them cook from twenty to thirty minutes; then drain, saving the water in which they were cooked. Make a sauce of 2 tablespoons of butter and 2 tablespoons of flour rubbed together, and 2 cups of the water in which the cucumbers were boiled, stir until smooth, and when it boils add the juice of 1 lemon, 1 teaspoon of salt, and some paprika; arrange the cucumbers on slices of toast and serve with the sauce poured over them.

STUFFED CUCUMBERS

Peel the cucumbers and cut into pieces about two inches long, scoop out the centre of each piece about half-way down to form a cup, fill this with chopped onions and chopped mushrooms that have been fried together in butter, cover the tops with crumbs, and let brown in the oven.

FRIED EGG-PLANT WITH SAUCE TARTARE

Peel and cut an egg-plant into half-inch slices, dust quickly with salt and pepper, roll in beaten egg-yolk, then in fine bread crumbs, and fry in hot vegetable fat; drain on brown paper and serve very hot. Either serve sauce Tartare with this, or arrange a spoonful on each round of egg-plant. Garnish with sprigs of watercress, celery tops, or parsley.

FRIED EGG-PLANT WITH TOMATO SAUCE

Fry as in foregoing recipe and serve a savoury tomato sauce with the egg-plant. Never soak egg-plant in salt and water, as it takes away its crispness.

CREAMED ENDIVE

Cut the outside leaves from heads of endive, and wash the endive thoroughly; then drain and put in boiling salted water for fifteen minutes. Drain again and cover with cold water for a few minutes, then chop and put in a saucepan with some butter, allowing 1 tablespoon for each head of endive, cover and let cook slowly for ten minutes, salt well, moisten with cream and sprinkle with paprika, and serve on toast or garnished with triangular pieces of toast.

KOHLRABI

These are very nice if used young, when not much larger than an egg. Parboil them for half an hour, cut them in half, and put them in a frying pan containing melted butter, and fry for fifteen or twenty minutes. Serve over them the butter in which they were cooked, and dredge with salt and pepper. The time required to cook kohlrabi depends largely of course upon the age at which it is picked.

KOHLRABI AU GRATIN

Slice kohlrabi, boil twenty minutes or until nearly tender, and arrange in a baking dish in layers with cream sauce. Season each layer with pepper and salt, sprinkle the top with crumbs and grated cheese, and bake twenty minutes.

LENTIL PIE

Put 1 tablespoon of butter in a saucepan, and when melted add to it 1 finely chopped onion and let this fry slowly for ten minutes; then add 2 cups of boiled German or Egyptian lentils and ½ cup of brown or German sauce, and when heated through pile into a deep dish; dredge with pepper and salt, cover with pie-crust, and bake in the oven until brown.

LENTILS EGYPTIAN STYLE

Wash 2 cups of lentils, soak them two or three hours, and drain them before using. Put them into boiling water well salted, cook until tender, about forty minutes, then drain again. Put 2 tablespoons of butter into a saucepan, and when melted add 1 large onion finely chopped; cook over a very slow fire for ten minutes, then add the lentils and 2 scant cups of boiled rice, and stir all together with a large fork until very hot; dredge well with salt and pepper before serving.

GERMAN LENTILS

Cover 2 cups of lentils with cold water and let them soak two or three hours; drain them and put them in boiling salted water with 1 leek (or 1 onion) and let them cook half an hour, or until tender but not broken. Put 2 tablespoons of butter in a frying pan, and when melted stir into it 2 tablespoons of flour, and let brown; then add 2 finely chopped onions and 2 or 3 tablespoons of vinegar and 2 tablespoons of the water in which the lentils cooked. Mix this sauce with the drained lentils, put them in a double boiler with salt, pepper, and a dash of nutmeg, and serve after they have steamed slowly for fifteen minutes.

LEEKS

Cut leeks into three-inch lengths, using the tender green part as well as the white; wash the pieces thoroughly in cold running water, then put them in a small saucepan and cover them with boiling salted water, and let them boil for twenty minutes.

Make a sauce by melting 1 tablespoon of butter and thickening it with 1 tablespoon of flour, and then adding, 1 tablespoon at a time, enough of the water the leeks were cooked in (about 1 cup) to make the sauce of the right consistency; season with pepper and salt, drain the leeks, and serve the sauce over them.

MUSHROOMS

Mushrooms should only be used when perfectly fresh and firm; in peeling them take a small knife, and, holding the delicate fringe at the edge of the mushroom between the edge of the knife and the thumb, peel the paper-like skin off, pulling it toward the centre of the mushroom. The stems should be cut or broken off without breaking the cup, and if sound should be scraped and used. When the mushrooms are white and small and freshly picked they can be quickly washed and used without peeling.

STEWED MUSHROOMS

Peel about 1 pound of mushrooms, put them in a saucepan with 2 tablespoons of butter, 1 saltspoon of pepper, 1 teaspoon of salt, and ¼ cup of milk, into which 1 tablespoon of flour has been mixed; cover and let cook for five or six minutes, then add 1 cup of cream, stir all well together, replace the cover, and let cook gently for ten minutes. These mushrooms can also be cooked and served in an Italian casserole.

GERMAN STEWED MUSHROOMS

Peel 1 pound of mushrooms and put them in a saucepan, sprinkle with the juice of 1 lemon, add 1 cup of milk, cover, and let simmer gently for ten minutes. Thicken with 1 heaping teaspoon of flour dissolved in a little milk, and add 1 tablespoon of butter and a grating of nutmeg, and let simmer gently for ten minutes more before serving. Instead of lemon juice and milk a cup of sour cream is often used in Germany, and is an acceptable substitute.

MUSHROOM AND CHESTNUT RAGOUT

Use an equal quantity of peeled mushrooms and boiled Italian chestnuts, and heat in a rich brown sauce. Serve, garnished with toast, or in cases, or use in a deep pie with a top crust of biscuit dough.

MUSHROOMS WITH ONIONS

Peel 2 medium-sized onions and chop them fine, and put them in a casserole, or saucepan, with 1 tablespoon of melted butter. Let them cook slowly for ten minutes, then add 1 pound of mushrooms, which have been carefully washed or peeled, and another tablespoon of butter, and cover, letting cook for ten minutes. Season well with salt and pepper and serve very hot.

Mushrooms thus prepared may be put in a deep baking dish, covered with crust and baked in a pie.

MUSHROOMS NEWBURG

Peel 1 pound of mushrooms, cover them with 2 cups of milk, and let them simmer gently for ten minutes. Lift the mushrooms out with a strainer, and make a sauce of the milk by adding 1 tablespoon of flour, 1 tablespoon of butter, the beaten yolks of 2 eggs, 1 wineglass of sherry, and some salt and paprika. When the sauce thickens replace the mushrooms in it, let them heat for two minutes, and serve on toast or in patty cases.

BAKED MUSHROOMS ON TOAST

Select as many large mushrooms as are required, and, after peeling them, lay each one, cup upward, on rounds of toast which, after toasting, have been dampened by being plunged quickly into hot water; place the toast with the mushrooms upon it into a shallow buttered pan, put a little bit of butter in the cup of each mushroom, sprinkle with salt and pepper, cover with another pan the same size, and let cook eight or ten minutes. Serve at once, with a garnish of parsley or watercress.

GRILLED MUSHROOMS

Peel or wash the mushrooms, and put them, cup upward, on a fine wire broiler and let them broil over a hot fire for five or six minutes, putting a pinch of salt in each cup. As soon as hot, remove them from the broiler and serve on hot plates, taking care not to spill the juice which has formed in the cups. Garnish with watercress or parsley.

MUSHROOMS SUR CLOCHE

Place carefully cleaned mushrooms, cup upward, on individual gratin dishes, salt each, and place a bit of butter in the cup, and set in a hot oven for ten minutes. To serve, place over each a glass "bell," which can be bought for this purpose. The heat is thus retained in the mushrooms during service.

MUSHROOMS IN CASSEROLE

Put into a French or Italian casserole ½ cup of good butter, and when melted stir into it ¾ of a pound, or a pound, of peeled mushrooms, and dredge well with pepper and salt. Cover the casserole and set it in the oven; after five minutes' cooking stir the mushrooms, mixing them well with the butter, replace the cover, and repeat the process in another five minutes; let cook ten minutes more, and serve from the casserole on rounds of toast.

FILLED MUSHROOMS

Select 10 of the largest, most cup-shaped from 1½ pounds of mushrooms. Peel and lay in a shallow pan, cup side up. Take the cleaned stems and the remaining mushrooms and chop fine and put them in the cups; add 1 teaspoon of melted butter, some pepper and salt to each, and let bake ten minutes or until done. Serve on toast garnished with watercress, or under the glass bells already mentioned.

MUSHROOMS WITH TRUFFLES

Toss truffles in butter in a hot frying pan for five minutes, sprinkle the cups of mushrooms with pepper and salt, fill them with the truffles, and cook for ten minutes in a covered pan in a hot oven; serve on crisp lettuce leaves, with parsley butter.

MUSHROOMS WITH PEAS

Fill the cups of large mushrooms with French canned peas, which have been tossed for five minutes in hot butter. Season and set in a covered pan in a hot oven for ten minutes, and serve on toast with white or brown sauce, as preferred.

MUSHROOMS WITH EGG

Put 2 tablespoons of butter in a porcelain casserole, or in a saucepan, and when melted put with it 1 pound of peeled or washed mushrooms; let simmer gently for ten minutes, then add to them 2 hard-boiled eggs, cut in slices, and half a cup of cream. This recipe also is available for a deep pie; put in a baking dish, cover with crust, and bake until slightly browned.

CANNED MUSHROOMS

Drain the mushrooms from 1 can, and cut them in half. Use the liquid from the can augmented with water, if necessary, to make brown or German sauce. Put the mushrooms in a saucepan with the sauce, season with pepper and salt, and serve very hot on toast.

Button mushrooms can also be cooked by simply draining and tossing in parsley butter until hot; season with salt and pepper and serve on toast.

Mushrooms cooked in these ways are suitable for filling peppers or tomatoes. Canned mushrooms can be bought which are put up with truffles, and add variety to these different dishes.

CANNED MUSHROOMS CZARINA

Open a can of button mushrooms, drain them, and cut the buttons in half, if very large, and reserve the liquid. Put 1 tablespoon of butter in a saucepan, and when melted add 1 tablespoon of grated onion, 2 bay leaves, 2 cloves, 2 peppercorns, and 2 allspice. Let all cook together slowly for five minutes, then pour on the liquid from the mushrooms, with enough milk added to make 2 cups, season with salt, and let simmer for ten minutes; then add 1 tablespoon of flour creamed with 1 tablespoon of butter, let boil up once, and strain. Put the sauce and the button mushrooms in an Italian casserole, set this in the oven to heat for five minutes, and serve from the dish on triangles of toast.

MUSHROOM LOAF

Pour good clear, well-strained boiling vegetable stock onto dissolved vegetable gelatine or arrowroot, using about 1 tablespoon to every 2 cups of liquid. Season well with salt and pepper, and add 1 can of button mushrooms, halved, when the jelly is somewhat set so that they will remain in place evenly dispersed. Line a mould with chopped parsley and slices of pickled walnuts, pour the jelly into it, and serve, when set, ice-cold, with any savoury cold sauce or pickles. A few chopped nuts may be added if desired.

STEWED OKRA

Cut the ends off the pods of young okra, boil for one hour in salted water, then drain and reheat in a saucepan with some melted butter.

The okra can be used as a garnish to boiled rice. Canned okra needs only to be boiled five minutes, drained, seasoned, and tossed about in hot butter in a frying pan for two or three minutes before serving.

OKRA AND GRILLED TOMATOES

Cut good firm tomatoes in half, season well and broil, then serve with a garnish of stewed okra.

STEWED OKRA WITH TOMATO SAUCE

If fresh okra is used prepare as in stewed okra recipe, and if canned okra is used drain and heat in boiling salted water. Put 1 tablespoon of butter in a frying pan, and when melted lift the okra from the boiling water and place it in the frying pan; season well with salt and pepper and then cover with 1 cup of tomato sauce, and, when thoroughly heated through, serve.

OKRA AND TOMATO ESCALLOP

Arrange alternate layers of sliced canned okra and tomato in a well buttered baking dish, separating them with layers of boiled rice well seasoned with salt and pepper and dotted with butter. Cover the top with fine crumbs and cook for fifteen minutes, or until browned, in the oven.

BOILED ONIONS

Peel onions under cold water and they will not bring tears to the eyes. They should then be put in rapidly boiling water, and this changed after the first five minutes of cooking; then put in fresh boiling water, salt added, and cooked for from half an hour to forty minutes. If onions are not covered when boiling the odour will be less noticeable.

Serve boiled onions with parsley butter, or, after draining, cover with milk, add butter, pepper, and salt, and let boil up once before serving.

CREAMED ONIONS

Use onions which have been boiled until tender but not broken, and, after draining, serve with white or parsley sauce, made with equal quantities of milk and the stock in which the onions cooked.

BOILED ONIONS WITH BROWN SAUCE

Serve small boiled onions, which have cooked until tender, but not broken, with any hot sauce,—tomato, brown, mushroom, etc.

ONIONS AU GRATIN

Prepare as for creamed onions, making a white sauce of the milk, or milk and water, in which the onions have been boiled. The onions can be left whole, or somewhat broken up in the sauce. Fill a buttered baking dish with onions and sauce, dust the top with grated cheese, and let heat in the oven five or six minutes. The bottled Parmesan cheese is convenient, but is never as delicate to the taste as fresh cheese grated.

ONIONS WITH CHEESE

Arrange boiled onions, which are not broken at all by boiling, in a buttered baking dish, baste well with melted butter, and dredge with grated cheese, and set in the oven a few moments to brown; serve in the same dish or remove to a small platter and garnish with green, or use as a garnish to a dish of other vegetables. Mashed potatoes piled high (browned on top with salamander or under flame in gas oven) surrounded with these onions makes an attractive dish.

ESCALLOPED ONIONS

Escalloped onions are made like Onions au Gratin, except that the cheese is omitted and replaced by a layer of fine bread crumbs.

BAKED ONIONS WITH CHESTNUTS

Peel as many onions as required and parboil them for ten or fifteen minutes in salted water. Drain and dry, and when cooled somewhat remove the inside and fill with chopped chestnuts which have been tossed in hot butter for fifteen minutes; season well with salt and pepper, and, if liked, a little sage; arrange in a buttered baking dish, and bake for half an hour, covering them for the first fifteen minutes. If they seem too dry, baste with a little cream or onion stock and melted butter.

ONION SOUFFLÉ

Put 1 tablespoon of butter in a saucepan, and when melted add 1 tablespoon of flour, stir until smooth, and then add gradually 1 cup of milk, and season with paprika and salt. Let boil, then add ½ cup of stale bread crumbs, 1 teaspoon of chopped parsley, 1½ cups of cold boiled onions chopped fine, and the yolks of 2 eggs well beaten. Mix thoroughly, then add the stiffly beaten whites of the 2 eggs, and mix them gently through the onion mixture with a fork. Put in a buttered baking dish, or in individual cases, sprinkle fine crumbs on top, and bake about fifteen minutes to slightly brown before serving.

BORDEAUX ONIONS

Peel 6 or 8 small onions, and parboil them for fifteen minutes in salted water. Put 2 tablespoons of butter in a saucepan or a baking dish, with 1 tablespoon of chopped parsley and 1 tablespoon of chopped celery, 2 cloves, 1 bay leaf, ¼ of a cup of claret,

1 cup of brown sauce, the juice of 1 lemon, pepper and salt. Set the onions in this, cover, and let cook very gently for half an hour or until tender. Remove the bay leaf and serve with the sauce.

ONION AND TOMATO ESCALLOP

Place alternate layers of fresh onions, sliced, and fresh tomatoes in a buttered baking dish, covering each layer with crumbs, butter, pepper and salt. Put 1½ cups of water over and bake for about an hour in a slow oven. Or use boiled onions and canned tomatoes, dampen with the juice from the tomatoes, and cook twenty minutes.

ONIONS BEATRICE

Fill a large bean-pot (or a high earthenware covered jar marmite) with small Bermuda onions, two inches in diameter. The onions should be left whole, but a sharp knife can be used to make two cuts in the shape of a cross in the top of each, as this insures the cooking of the centre. While arranging the onions in the jar, sprinkle them well with salt, also with black pepper (or use ½ dozen peppercorns instead), put in 3 bay leaves, and distribute 1 teaspoon of mixed herbs. Cover with hot water, put the lid on, and set on the back of the stove or in a slow oven. The onions should not cook to pieces, and with the proper heat will be cooked through in about two hours; this time is named not as a rule but as a guide. Serve in the marmite in which they were cooked.

STUFFED ONIONS

Boil the onions fifteen or twenty minutes and then remove the hearts, leaving the outsides as cases for a filling. Make the stuffing of bread or cracker crumbs mixed with the chopped centres of the onions, plenty of salt and pepper, and a little chopped tomato (or tomato sauce), or some chopped green peppers, or canned pimentos, or use both tomato and peppers. Fill the onion cases, and arrange in a buttered baking dish; sprinkle with 2 tablespoons of melted butter, set the pan in water, and bake half an hour; the baking dish should be covered until the last five minutes, and the onions should not be allowed to go dry; more butter can be added, or a little hot water or vegetable broth, if they cook dry. Serve in the baking dish, or remove to a small platter and garnish with sprigs of parsley.

FRIED ONIONS

Peel the onions and cut into thin slices, and when a generous tablespoon of butter has slowly melted in a frying pan, put the onions in and let them simmer over as low a fire as will keep them cooking; stir them frequently and serve when transparent and turning a golden brown.

Fried onions can be served alone or as a garnish to heaped up mashed potatoes. They are saved from their extreme commonplaceness by being arranged in a gratin dish, not over an inch high, dusted with a sprinkling of crumbs or grated cheese, and given three or four minutes in the oven.

FRENCH FRIED ONIONS

Peel medium-sized onions, and slice crosswise carefully; then separate the slices into rings. Drop these into smoking vegetable fat or oil, and let fry four or five minutes until crisp and a rich brown. Lift with a strainer onto brown paper to drain a moment before serving.

ONIONS IN POTATO CRADLES

Make potato cradles as directed, dredge with salt, and fill with fried or French-fried onions.

SMALL ONIONS

Peel small, round, pickling onions, parboil them ten minutes, drain, roll in flour, and fry in deep fat. Serve as a garnish to other vegetables or in stews.

GLAZED ONIONS

These are nice used either as a garnish to another dish (vegetable croquettes, mashed potatoes, etc.) or alone. Small onions should be used, or onion hearts, and taken from the water before they are quite cooked; then put in an enamelled pan in which is 1 tablespoon of butter which has been slowly melted; toss them about in this, and sprinkle with powdered sugar. When they begin to brown add 1 tablespoon of the water in which they were boiled, and as this is taken up add a little more, and pepper and salt. The onions will be browned and glazed. Serve very hot.

ONIONS AND APPLES

Put 1 tablespoon of butter in a frying pan, and when melted put in 3 sliced onions and 3 sliced apples; let fry slowly until browned, and serve on toast.

BOILED PARSNIPS IN SAUCE

Wash and scrape 6 or 7 parsnips, cut them in half, lengthwise, and put them in cold water for half an hour. Drain them, and put them in a saucepan of boiling water containing 1 teaspoon of salt, and let them boil for about three quarters of an hour. While they are finishing cooking, prepare a sauce with 1 tablespoon of butter and 1 tablespoon of flour rubbed together, and put in a saucepan over a slow fire. When melted and smooth add, a spoonful at a time, some of the stock in which the parsnips are cooking, until about 2 cups have been used; stir until well thickened but not paste-like, season with salt and pepper, and pour over the parsnips after draining them.

PARSNIPS IN BUTTER

Scrape and wash the parsnips, and cut them in eighths, lengthwise, and then in half. Put them in boiling water, salt well, and let them cook for about three quarters of an hour. Drain and serve with ½ cup melted butter poured over them, which contains 1 tablespoon of chopped parsley.

FRIED PARSNIPS

Slice cold boiled parsnips lengthwise, dredge with salt, and fry in buttered pan or griddle until a golden brown, turning with a pancake turner.

FRENCH FRIED PARSNIPS

Use cold boiled parsnips, cut in any shape desired,—balls, or long strips,—and put them in a frying basket, and fry in hot fat until brown. Drain, and dredge with salt to serve.

BROILED PARSNIPS

Use boiled parsnips, cut each in 3 slices, lengthwise, dip in melted butter, broil until brown, and sprinkle with salt before serving.

GREEN PEAS

Newly picked green peas should be shelled and put in a double-boiler with a little salt, and 1 teaspoon or more of sugar, and no water. Cover closely and keep water in under pan boiling for about three quarters of an hour. Add a little butter before serving.

GREEN PEAS PAYSANNE

Cook peas as in the above recipe adding a few lettuce leaves which have been washed and cut in strips. Drain them before adding butter and salt.

CANNED PEAS

Canned peas should be slowly cooked in their own stock for ten minutes, drained, and seasoned with butter, pepper and salt, and a little milk or cream added to them.

CANNED PEAS WITH ONION

Put 1 tablespoon of butter in a saucepan, and when melted add 1 tablespoon of chopped onion; let simmer for five minutes, then add 1 can of peas, drained of their juice, and ¼ of a cup of cream or milk; season well with salt and pepper, and serve after ten minutes' slow cooking.

STUFFED PEPPERS

Slice the stem-end from sweet peppers, cut out the insides, and fill with a mixture made of 1 cup of fine crumbs, 1 grated onion, ½ cup of chopped nuts, 1 teaspoon of salt, and 2 tablespoons of melted butter. Set in a pan containing a little water and melted butter, and bake from twenty minutes to half an hour, basting occasionally.

Peppers can be parboiled for ten minutes before stuffing, but though softer they lose their colour to some extent.

PEPPERS STUFFED WITH MUSHROOMS

Cut the stem-end from sweet peppers, remove the inside, and fill with mushrooms Czarina, or mushrooms in tomato sauce, and bake twenty to thirty minutes, basting with a little butter and water, which should be in the pan in which they are cooked.

PEPPERS WITH RICE

Cut the stem-end from sweet green peppers, remove the inside, fill with boiled rice and chopped tomato in equal proportions, and season well with pepper and salt. A few chopped mushrooms, olives, or boiled eggs may be added to the filling. Bake from twenty to thirty minutes, basting with butter and water.

GREEN PEPPERS WITH EGG

Parboil 6 green peppers for five minutes, first having cut off the stem-end and removed the seeds. Put 2 tablespoons of butter in a frying pan, and when melted add 1 finely chopped onion, and let it cook slowly for ten minutes; then stir in 3 tablespoons of fine bread crumbs, and season with salt, pepper, and catsup. Upon removing the peppers from the boiling water set them up cup-like in a shallow pan, and put 1 tablespoon of this mixture into each; break into each pepper 1 egg, cover with some more of the prepared crumbs, and bake for ten minutes if the eggs are liked soft, for fifteen if liked hard. Serve on toast with 1½ cups of white sauce containing 2 tablespoons of grated cheese.

PEPPERS WITH CORN

Cut a slice from the end of sweet peppers, remove the inside, and fill with canned corn, well salted; replace the ends and bake.

Peppers, like tomatoes, may be filled in so many ways that it is useless to endeavour to enumerate them, for the ingenious cook can multiply them without end.

ESCALLOP OF PEPPERS AND CORN

Cut enough sweet corn from the cob to make 3 cups. Take 2 or 3 sweet green peppers and remove the insides, then slice them in very thin circles and arrange a layer of the corn in a buttered baking dish, salt it, and then place some rings of the peppers, then another layer of corn, and so on, until the dish is filled, finishing the top with peppers. To a cup of cream (or milk) add 1 beaten egg and 2 tablespoons of melted butter; pour this over the whole, and bake for half an hour in a hot oven. Canned corn may be used, in which case less cream will be needed.

FRIED PEPPERS

Remove the seeds from 6 sweet green peppers, cut the pods in squares about half an inch across. Put 1 tablespoon of butter in a frying pan, and when melted add 1 sliced onion, and let simmer for two or three minutes; then put into the pan the cut-up peppers, and fry for ten minutes. Add ½ cup of brown or tomato sauce and serve on toast with boiled rice, or on flat rice cakes.

CREAMED PIMENTOS

Put the pimentos from 1 can into 2 cups of white sauce, and let cook in a double boiler for ten minutes. Add 1 tablespoon of chopped parsley, some pepper and salt, and serve on toast.

ROLLED PIMENTOS

Remove the pimentos from the can, and with a sharp knife cut them open on one side and open them out. Arrange the flat pieces thus made on a large plate or board, with the inner part up, and spread with finely chopped onion, sprinkle with salt and celery salt, and roll into firm rolls. Place these in a well-buttered tin, add a little hot water, cover, and set in a hot oven for ten minutes; then uncover, add 1 tablespoon of butter, and when it melts baste the pimentos with it. Let them cook five minutes more, and serve with the melted butter poured over them, or with parsley butter.

PIMENTOS WITH OKRA

Split the pimentos with a sharp knife, salt the inner part, then roll each around a pod of freshly boiled or canned okra. Place in a well-buttered pan, add a little hot water, and let cook ten minutes covered, and five uncovered. Add more butter during the last five minutes, baste the rolls, and serve with the butter poured over them, or with tomato sauce.

PIMENTOS WITH TOMATO

Lay the large flat pimentos from a can on a platter, and slide into each a slice of tomato which has been sprinkled with salt and celery salt. Fry in a covered pan for five minutes, and serve plain or with caper sauce.

POTATOES

Between the good cooks who contend that a potato is never properly "boiled" if it is boiled at all, and those who either cook potatoes in a steamer, or put them in cold water which is carefully watched to see that it does not actually boil, cooking thus until the potatoes are tender, and those who drop them into rapidly boiling salted water, letting them boil hard until done, there is wide latitude for individual preference. I would advise those who do not have potatoes served on the table which are white and floury and thoroughly cooked through, to see that one of the above-mentioned ways of cooking potatoes is carried out in their kitchens. Potatoes put in boiling water, or put in a covered steamer over rapidly boiling water, will cook in from twenty minutes to half an hour, the time depending, of course, upon the size and age of the potatoes; they should always be carefully scrubbed and cooked in their skins, and peeled afterwards.

MASHED POTATOES

Having boiled or steamed the required number of potatoes, peel them as expeditiously as possible and break them up in a hot saucepan; mash and then beat them vigorously with a wooden spoon or a fork, add a generous piece of butter, dredge with salt and a little pepper, and beat them until they are light; then moisten slightly with a very little hot milk or cream, beat them for a moment more, and serve very hot.

POTATO SOUFFLÉ

Put into a saucepan 3 or 4 cups of warm mashed potato and 1 tablespoon butter. Add the yolks of 2 eggs, 2 tablespoons cream (or milk), salt and pepper, and stir over fire until well mixed. Remove from the fire and add the well-beaten whites of the eggs. Heap in a buttered baking dish and let brown on the top in the oven.

MASHED POTATO SOUFFLÉ IN CASES

Select large potatoes, scrub them and let them bake until mealy, which will be in from half an hour to three quarters, then cut them in half, lengthwise, and carefully scrape out the potato, laying aside the skins to use as cases. Mash the potatoes with a wire potato-masher, add 1 tablespoon of butter for every 5 potatoes used, and season well with salt and pepper. Beat the whites of eggs very stiff, allowing 2 to every 5 potatoes, and mix them lightly through the potato with a fork; fill the potato skins with the mixture, heaping them full; brown them slightly in the oven before serving, and garnish the dish on which they are served with sprigs of parsley. Five potatoes will fill 6 or 7 cases.

RICED POTATOES

Break up well-boiled dry potatoes with a fork, dredge with salt and pepper, and press through a sieve or a so-called "ricer" into a hot serving dish.

RICED POTATO FRITTERS

Boil 6 large potatoes, press them through a sieve, and add 3 lightly beaten eggs, 2 teaspoons of flour creamed with 1 tablespoon of butter, 1 teaspoon of salt, and 2 cups of milk. Beat well together, and drop from a large spoon into deep, hot fat; they will rise to the top a light brown when done. Chopped chives or chopped parsley may be added to the mixture if desired.

MASHED POTATOES WITH ONION

To 4 or 5 cups of mashed potato add 1 cup of boiled onion minced to a pulp, 1 tablespoon of butter, 1 tablespoon of cream, some pepper and salt; beat lightly together, and before serving brown the top for a moment in the oven.

BAKED POTATOES

Select potatoes of uniform size, scrub them well, place in a hot oven until they yield to pressure of the fingers, which will be in most cases in about three quarters of an hour. They should not stand after baking, and should be served in an open dish. A baked potato that is worked with the fingers while being turned in the hand a few times, becomes light and soft.

ROAST POTATOES

Pare small, round potatoes, and lay them in cold water. Put 2 tablespoons of butter in a shallow baking pan, and let it melt in the oven; then wipe the potatoes, and lay them in the pan, rolling each in the hot butter. Let them cook in a moderate oven from one half to three quarters of an hour, and baste them during the cooking five or six times with the butter. Sprinkle with salt before serving.

DENVER POTATOES

Peel several smooth oval potatoes and cut in half, lengthwise. Dig out a small hole in the centre of the smooth side, and level the rounded parts so they will sit evenly. Put a lump of butter in each, and place in a pan with a little water, first dredging with salt and pepper, and bake about twenty-five minutes or until browned.

BROILED POTATOES

Cut cold boiled potatoes lengthwise into quarter-inch slices, dip each in flour, and lay in a folding broiler. Broil until evenly browned on both sides, sprinkle with salt and pepper, and serve on a hot dish with a bit of butter on each, or as a garnish to other vegetables.

FRIED POTATOES SOUFFLÉ

Peel and trim the required number of potatoes to a uniform size, cut both ends straight across, and then slice the potatoes into slices about 1/16 of an inch thick, and drop them into cold water for about half an hour, and then dry them with a cloth. For the frying two kettles of fat are necessary, one of which must be perfectly fresh; drop the potatoes into the used fat or oil and let them fry until about half done; but do not let them brown at all; drain them thoroughly and let them get cold. Five or six minutes before they are to be served drop them into the fresh fat which should be almost smoking, move them about lightly with a fork, and they will puff out to a considerable size; let them become a golden brown, put them in the oven on brown paper for a moment, and serve instantly.

WHOLE POTATOES FRIED

Use very small new potatoes, and, after boiling them, roll in egg and cracker crumbs, and fry in hot, deep fat. Use alone or as a garnish to baked tomatoes.

FRENCH-FRIED POTATOES

Peel potatoes which are of medium size and cut into even eighths, lengthwise, and then let them lie in cold water for fifteen minutes; then dry them between the folds of a clean cloth, and put in a frying basket. Immerse slowly in hot fat, and fry until a golden brown; drain at once, and dredge with salt.

SARATOGA CHIPS

Cut potatoes into thin slices with a potato cutter, lay in cold water twenty minutes, dry, and fry in deep, hot fat until crisp. Drain from the fat onto brown paper, dredge with salt, and serve very hot.

POTATOES PARISIAN

These are cooked exactly like French-fried potatoes, except that the little vegetable cutter, which cuts tiny globes of potato, is used to form the shapes. Some care must be taken to use strength enough with the cutter to make it cut perfectly round balls.

POTATO STRAWS

Peel 4 or 5 potatoes and then cut them with a patent vegetable cutter in strings; lay them in very cold water for twenty minutes, drain, and put in a frying basket, and slowly immerse in hot fat, and let them fry until a golden brown. Drain, and dredge with salt before serving.

POTATO CRADLES

Peel, wash, and dry potatoes of uniform size and shape. Cut in two, lengthwise, and scoop out the inside, and fry the potato cases in hot fat until brown; then drain and sprinkle with salt. Serve hot peas heaped up in each cradle and garnish with mint or parsley.

POTATOES LYONNAISE

Take 5 or 6 cold boiled potatoes and cut them in slices. Put 1 tablespoon of butter in a frying pan, and when it is melted add 2 thinly sliced, medium-sized onions, and fry these, letting them cook very slowly ten minutes; then season with pepper and salt and add the sliced potatoes, and let these fry slowly, turning with a knife until they are a golden brown; season afresh with pepper and salt, and add 1 tablespoon of finely chopped parsley before serving. These potatoes will take a great deal of salt and pepper.

GERMAN FRIED POTATOES

Put 1 tablespoon of butter in a frying pan, and when melted add 5 or 6 cold boiled potatoes cut in slices, season highly with salt and pepper, fry until done, which will be about twelve or fifteen minutes, turning with a knife; when nearly done stop stirring, and let the potatoes brown on the bottom of the pan; serve in a hot dish with the browned slices on the top.

FRIED POTATO SAVOURY

Fry cold sliced or diced potatoes, and when browned add ½ teaspoon of onion juice or extract, then arrange in a buttered baking dish in layers with grated cheese, pepper, salt, and some butter in each layer, cover the top with a few brown crumbs and chopped parsley or chives, and let heat a few minutes in the oven. Chopped chives can be arranged with the layers of potato if the flavour is liked.

CREAMED POTATOES

Put 2 tablespoons of butter into a saucepan, and when melted add 1 tablespoon of minced parsley and pepper and salt, stir until very hot, then add a scant cup of milk, containing 1 teaspoon of flour and a pinch of soda, and when this boils add diced cold boiled potatoes, and, when thoroughly heated through, serve.

ESCALLOPED POTATOES

Boil 10 or 12 medium-sized potatoes in their skins, and after peeling slice them in slices ¼ of an inch thick. While the potatoes are boiling make a sauce of 2 cups of milk, the juice of 1 onion, salt and pepper, 2 tablespoons of butter, and 1 tablespoon of thickening flour. Butter a baking dish, and arrange a layer of potatoes, cover with sauce, then put another layer of potatoes, and so continue until the dish is filled. Then cut 2 hard-boiled eggs in neat slices, arrange them over the top, sprinkle with cracker crumbs and a little finely chopped parsley, and cook ten or twelve minutes in the oven.

POTATOES DELMONICO

For a large baking dish 4 cups of cold boiled diced potatoes will be required. Butter a baking dish, and put a layer of potatoes an inch deep in the bottom, and cover this with well made white sauce, and sprinkle slightly with salt and pepper; then add another layer of potato, and white sauce, and seasoning, and so on, until the dish is heaping full, and then sprinkle the top with grated cheese, and let brown well in a hot oven.

OAK HILL POTATOES

Butter a baking dish well, and place in it alternate layers of sliced cold boiled potatoes and hard-boiled eggs, seasoning each layer; then pour over it a white sauce in which grated cheese is melted. Cover the top of the dish with cracker crumbs, and brown in the oven.

HEILBRONN POTATOES

Put 2 tablespoons of butter in a deep saucepan, and when melted stir into it, with a flat-ended wooden spoon, 2 tablespoons of flour and let brown, then add 2 tablespoons of vinegar and use 2 cups of boiling water or vegetable stock in making this into a smooth sauce. Add ½ an onion, sliced, 2 cloves, 2 allspice, a piece of thin lemon peel, 1 tablespoon of lemon juice, and let cook very slowly, stirring for ten minutes. Then add more vegetable stock or boiling water to make a thin sauce and strain it; return to the fire and add 5 or 6 parboiled thinly sliced potatoes, 2 tablespoons of capers, and let cook slowly for fifteen minutes, stirring frequently; then pour into the saucepan ½ cup of cream (sour preferred), and serve in a deep, hot dish.

SAVOURY POTATO CAKES

Chop 6 cold boiled potatoes, and crush with a potato masher (or use cold mashed potato); add to them 1 tablespoon of mixed herbs, 1 teaspoon of chopped onions, pepper, salt, 1 tablespoon of melted butter, and 1 beaten egg; mould into flat cakes, and put in a frying pan containing 1 tablespoon of melted butter; brown, and turn with a pancake turner to brown the other side.

POTATO HASH

Put 8 cold boiled potatoes and 2 medium-sized onions in a chopping bowl and chop them fine. Melt 1 tablespoon of butter in a large frying pan, place the potatoes and onion in it, and smooth the top even with a fork. Season well with salt and pepper and put over a moderately hot fire, shaking the pan vigorously from time to time to keep the hash from burning. If it is shaken instead of being stirred it will brown well on the bottom. Turn out onto a hot serving dish, with the browned part on top, and sprinkle with salt and pepper.

POTATO OMELET

Butter a frying pan with 1 teaspoon of butter, and cover the bottom of the pan with sliced cold boiled potatoes laid flat; let these fry a few moments, then pour over them 2 well-beaten eggs and 1 tablespoon of chopped parsley or chives, season well with salt and pepper, and turn from the pan when browned.

CURRIED POTATOES

Chop 1 good-sized onion very fine, and fry in 2 tablespoons of butter until transparent and cooked, but not brown; then remove most of the onion with a strainer, pressing the juice from it into the butter, and put in 4 or 5 sliced cold boiled potatoes; sprinkle some curry powder and salt and pepper over them and fry, turning them frequently until done. The amount of curry can vary from 1 to 2 teaspoons.

POTATO FRICASSEE

Put in a saucepan 1 generous tablespoon of butter and 1 cup of milk; when hot add some cold potatoes cut in dice, season with pepper, salt, and a few drops of onion juice. Let them get thoroughly hot, then add the beaten yolks of 2 eggs, stir constantly until thick. Great care must be taken not to let it cook too long or the sauce will curdle. Add a little chopped parsley before serving.

POTATOES RENNEQUIN

Boil 6 potatoes, peel them, and let them dry in a warm place on the stove. Put 1 tablespoon of butter into a saucepan, and when partly melted slice the potatoes into it. Now add 1 tablespoon of water, some salt, pepper, and 1 tablespoon of minced parsley; let it become thoroughly heated, then add 1 tablespoon of lemon juice and serve very hot.

POTATOES AND CHEESE

Mince or chop fine 5 or 6 peeled raw potatoes, and toss in a saucepan with 2 tablespoons of butter until cooked. Place a layer of these in a buttered baking dish, season with salt and pepper, and sprinkle with grated cheese; then add another layer of potatoes, and proceed thus until the dish is full. Pour melted butter over and let brown in the oven.

ESCALLOPED POTATO AND ONION

Peel and slice very thinly 5 or 6 medium-sized potatoes and 3 or 4 onions, and arrange them in layers in a buttered baking dish, dotting them with butter, and sprinkling with pepper and salt. Over all pour ½ cup of milk, or enough to dampen well, and almost cover, and set the dish in a shallow pan containing a little water, and let the escallop cook slowly for about an hour, keeping it covered for the first half-hour, and uncovered afterward to brown. Serve in the baking dish.

NEW POTATOES IN BUTTER

Scrub small new potatoes with a stiff brush, and boil or steam them for twenty-five minutes, and serve them with melted butter to which a teaspoon or more of finely chopped parsley has been added.

CREAMED NEW POTATOES

Scrub small new potatoes with a stiff brush which will remove the skins, and boil or steam them about twenty-five minutes; then cover them with a highly seasoned white sauce.

BAKED NEW POTATOES

Scrub the skin from small new potatoes, and cook in salted boiling water about twenty minutes or until tender. Make a white sauce of 1 tablespoon of flour, 1 tablespoon butter, and 1 cup of milk seasoned highly with salt and pepper, and, after arranging the boiled potatoes in a baking dish or casserole, pour the sauce over them, and on the top of all pour 1 well-beaten egg. Put the dish in the oven and let it stay just long enough to set the egg. Sprinkle with chopped parsley before sending to the table. If preferred the egg can be added to the white sauce instead of being put on top.

MOCK NEW POTATOES

Peel the required number of large old potatoes, and with a Parisian potato cutter cut them into small balls; drop these in boiling water, and when done cover with a highly seasoned white sauce, to which is added a very little chopped parsley.

BOILED SWEET POTATOES

As the skin of sweet potatoes does not come off well after cooking it is best to peel them before baking or boiling.

Select large sweet potatoes, put them in boiling water, and let them boil from half to three quarters of an hour. Peel them and arrange them in a hot dish, with ½ cup of melted butter poured over them.

BAKED SWEET POTATOES

Wash and peel the sweet potatoes and put them in the oven. A medium-sized potato will take about forty minutes to bake.

MASHED SWEET POTATOES

Peel and boil 6 or 7 sweet potatoes, drain off all the water, and then mash with a wire potato-masher in the saucepan in which they were cooked; mix with them while hot 2 tablespoons of good butter, and dredge generously with salt, and serve very hot.

SWEET POTATO SOUFFLÉ

Mix with mashed sweet potatoes when slightly cooled the beaten yolks of 2 eggs and then the stiff whites of the eggs. Heap in a buttered baking dish and let brown in the oven.

ESCALLOPED SWEET POTATOES

Slice what will make 4 or 5 cups of cold boiled sweet potatoes, butter a baking dish, and arrange a layer of potatoes in the bottom, making it an inch thick. Sprinkle with salt, pepper, and dot well with butter. Then arrange another layer, proceed as before, and so on until the dish is filled. Then pour over all ½ cup of water in which 2 tablespoons of sugar are dissolved. Put the dish in the oven, and in ten minutes baste with 2 tablespoons of water. Let cook five minutes more or until browned on top.

STUFFED SWEET POTATOES

Bake in their skins the number of potatoes required, cut them in half, scoop out the inside, and mix with chopped celery, and minced onion, and melted butter, allowing 1 tablespoon of celery and ½ teaspoon of onion to each potato. Season with salt and pepper, refill the skins, and let brown in the oven.

SOUTHERN SWEET POTATO PIE

Bake 4 large sweet potatoes, then scrape the inside from them, and beat into it lightly with a fork 2 tablespoons of butter, 2 tablespoons of sugar, 3 well-beaten eggs, 1 cup of warm milk, a saltspoon of salt, and a pinch of mixed spice. Line a baking dish with pastry, fill with the potato, and bake for twenty minutes.

TEXAS SWEET POTATO PIE

Boil 4 or 5 sweet potatoes for half an hour or until cooked. Line a large baking dish with pie-crust, slice the potatoes lengthwise while still hot, and put a layer of them on the crust, and cover this with long strips of pastry. Sprinkle with sugar, dot with butter, and add a little nutmeg; then place another layer of potato, and another of pastry, and so on, until the dish is nearly filled. Pour on enough boiling water to almost fill the dish, and cover the top with pastry like any deep pie, cutting it here and there to let the steam escape. Bake for about twenty minutes, or until the crust is a little browned.

MARYLAND SWEET POTATOES

Peel 6 or 8 medium-sized sweet potatoes, quarter them lengthwise, and lay them in a large saucepan having rounded sides. Add to the potatoes 2 heaping tablespoons of butter, and 3 heaping tablespoons of granulated sugar, and 2 or 3 tablespoons of water, and stir until the sugar and butter are dissolved. Cover closely and let them cook for four or five minutes undisturbed, then stir again with a wooden spoon, being careful to see that the syrup is not sticking on the bottom, re-cover, and from now on let cook only a couple of moments at a time before again stirring. The water will of course soon cook away; let the potatoes cook rapidly in the hot syrup until they begin to soften, then put them where the fire is less hot, and let them cook slowly until done. The entire cooking should not take more than fifteen or twenty minutes, and the thick brown sauce should be thoroughly scraped from the saucepan and served over the sweet potatoes.

CANDIED SWEET POTATOES

Lay pared sweet potatoes cut in slices in a buttered baking dish with a cover. Sprinkle each layer with brown sugar, salt and pepper and cinnamon, and dot with bits of butter. Pour in ½ cup of boiling water for ½ dozen potatoes and baste while cooking. Cook moderately until tender, from half an hour to three quarters, depending on the heat of the oven. The cinnamon can be omitted if not liked.

GRIDDLED SWEET POTATOES

Cut cold boiled sweet potatoes in slices, lengthwise, and lay them on a buttered griddle; when browned on one side turn with a pancake turner and brown the other side. Sprinkle with salt and serve very hot.

FRIED SWEET POTATOES

Cut cold boiled sweet potatoes in half-inch squares and fry them in melted butter. Salt well, and stir with a knife, and let brown as much as possible without burning.

FRENCH-FRIED SWEET POTATOES

Cut cold boiled sweet potatoes in sixths, lengthwise, place in a frying basket, and fry for about five minutes, or until well browned. Drain and sprinkle with salt.

GLAZED SWEET POTATOES

Let sweet potatoes boil until nearly done, then drain and cool. When cold cut them in inch-thick slices, or into rounds with a patent cutter, mix them well with melted butter and sugar, using 2 tablespoons of sugar to each ½ cup of butter, and put them in a deep dish in a hot oven for ten minutes, or until well browned.

CREAMED SALSIFY (OYSTER PLANT)

Remove the tops from 2 bunches of salsify, scrape and cut to shape, and put in a bowl of cold water containing some lemon juice, to retain the whiteness. Drain and put in boiling water, using enough to cover it, and let cook about three quarters of an hour, salting the water during the last half-hour's boiling. Drain and serve with highly seasoned white sauce or parsley sauce made with the water in which the salsify cooked, with the addition of a little milk or cream.

ENGLISH SALSIFY

Boil salsify as directed above, drain, and serve with bread sauce, serving fine browned bread crumbs with the sauce.

SALSIFY IN COQUILLES

Boil the salsify as directed, and press through a sieve; then beat into it 1 tablespoon of butter, season highly, arrange in buttered coquilles or ramekins, sprinkle grated cheese over the top, and let brown in the oven.

ESCALLOPED SALSIFY

Boil salsify as directed, not letting it quite finish cooking; slice, and arrange in buttered baking dish, with layers of slightly browned crumbs dotted with butter, and sprinkled with pepper, salt, and paprika. Pour ½ cup of milk or cream over to dampen, then cover the top with crumbs, and bake about fifteen minutes. An egg can be beaten with the milk to make the dish richer if wanted.

MASHED BLACK SALSIFY (SCHWARZWURZEL)

Proceed as with ordinary salsify, except that it is best not to peel or cut this sort of salsify until after boiling. When boiled, peel, and mash the white part, using 1 tablespoon of cream to each cup of salsify, 1 teaspoon of butter, pepper, and salt. Arrange in individual dishes or cases with crumbs on top, and bake ten minutes to brown.

FRIED SALSIFY TARTARE

Use cold boiled salsify, cut in any shape desired, dip in egg and crumbs, and fry in hot fat until browned. Drain well, dredge with salt, and serve with sauce Tartare.

SPINACH

Spinach should be well picked over, leaf by leaf, and washed in several different waters, and changed to a different pan each time it is washed, that the sand may be left behind with each washing. Then put it in a large kettle, with a scant cup of water for a peck of spinach, and let it cook over a slow fire until tender; in this way its own juices will be extracted, and it will be more tasty than if cooked in water. It should be then drained and chopped extremely fine, or until as nearly a pulp as possible, and then mashed in a mortar or with a potato-masher. It is then ready to prepare in any way desired for the table.

Delicious spinach can be had canned, and if this is used it needs only to be very finely chopped and mashed, then seasoned, and prepared in any of the following ways.

GERMAN SPINACH

Melt 1 tablespoon of butter in a saucepan, and in it let simmer for ten minutes 1 good-sized onion that has been finely chopped, then add 4 cups of the boiled, chopped, and mashed spinach to it, and stir well together, and season thoroughly with salt and pepper; finish with ½ teaspoon of grated nutmeg, and 1 or 2 tablespoons of whipped cream, and pile high in a heated dish, covering the top with the chopped whites and riced yolks of 2 hard-boiled eggs.

SPINACH WITH WHITE SAUCE

Prepare as in the above recipe, using, instead of the cream, ½ cup of highly seasoned white sauce, and at the last add the juice of 1 lemon or 1 tablespoon of reduced vinegar.

GERMAN SPINACH WITH RHUBARB

Another German way of preparing spinach is to cook rhubarb leaves or flowers (or both) with the spinach for the purée and to add chives. If canned spinach is used the rhubarb leaves should be cooked and chopped and added to the canned spinach before it is macerated.

ITALIAN SPINACH

Wash ½ peck spinach and cook twenty-five minutes without water. Drain, chop to a fine pulp, mash until smooth in a mortar, season with 1 tablespoon of butter, salt and pepper, and encircle with a garnish of well-scrambled eggs to which has been added 2 tablespoons of grated cheese.

NOVELTY SPINACH

Drain a can of spinach and chop it very fine, and then mash it until smooth. Put it in a saucepan with 1 tablespoon of chopped chives or grated onion, salt and pepper, and sprinkle the whole surface well with grated nutmeg. Hard boil 3 eggs, remove the yolks, and mix them thoroughly with the spinach. Chop the whites, and arrange the spinach on rounds of toast, placing 2 tablespoons on each piece, garnish with the whites of the eggs, and pour on each 2 tablespoons of cheese sauce. If the arrangement on toast is not desired, the cheese sauce can be mixed with the spinach before serving it.

SPINACH SOUFFLÉ

Take 2 cups of cooked chopped spinach, mash to a pulp, add 1 cup of white sauce and the whites of 2 eggs beaten very stiff, season well, and pile lightly in timbale cups; set these in a pan of water, and let bake in a moderate oven for fifteen minutes or less. Before serving sprinkle the top of each with riced yolk of hard-boiled egg.

BAKED SQUASH OR PUMPKIN

Cut a pumpkin or a squash in triangular or square pieces, about three inches across, scrape the seeds, etc., from each piece, and sprinkle with salt and pepper, and spread with butter. Set in a moderate oven and bake for half an hour or until browned. Serve garnished with sprigs of parsley. It should be eaten from the shell with additional butter.

CALIFORNIA SQUASH

Take a very young summer squash, which if it be young enough need not be pared, and cut it into small pieces. Fry half an onion in a tablespoon of butter, and when transparent and beginning to brown add the squash to it and season with salt and pepper. Let all cook together for ten minutes, and then add ¼ of a cup of hot water, and let cook until the squash is quite tender.

STEWED TOMATOES

Empty 1 can of tomatoes into a double boiler, and put with them 1 cup of crumbled bread without crust, stir well together, season with pepper and salt, cover, and let cook slowly for half an hour, stirring from time to time. Just before serving add a piece of butter the size of a walnut. While the tomatoes will be ready to serve with half an hour's cooking, they are improved by cooking an hour, and are better still if warmed again after cooling.

ESCALLOPED TOMATOES

Drain the juice from 1 can of tomatoes. Butter a baking dish, and cover the bottom with the tomatoes; dot with butter, dredge with pepper and salt, and sprinkle generously with fine bread crumbs; arrange another layer of tomatoes, and crumbs, and so proceed until the dish is filled. Pour over all enough of the juice of the tomatoes to moisten well, and then finish the dish with a covering of crumbs. Bake for twenty minutes in a moderate oven.

BREADED TOMATOES

Slice large, solid tomatoes, dredge them on both sides with salt and pepper, and dip each slice in beaten egg, and then in fine bread or cracker crumbs. Arrange them in a frying basket, and plunge them in hot, deep fat for one or two minutes to brown. Drain, and garnish with sprays of parsley, or use as a garnish to other vegetables.

FRIED TOMATOES

Put 1 tablespoon of butter in a frying pan, and when melted lay in thickly sliced tomatoes which have been rolled in egg and crumbs; when browned on one side turn them with a pancake turner and brown the other side, seasoning with pepper and salt. Remove to the serving dish with a pancake turner, seasoning the first side cooked after they are turned onto the dish. A half a teaspoon of onion juice may be added to the butter in which they are cooking if desired. Serve plain or with white sauce.

DEVILLED TOMATOES

Cut in half and broil three or four nice solid tomatoes, and serve them with a sauce made as follows: Take the yolks of 4 hard-boiled eggs and crush them with a fork, add to them a scant teaspoon of dry mustard, 1 heaping saltspoon of salt, and several shakes of paprika, or a dash of cayenne pepper; mix these dry ingredients well together, and then add to them 5 tablespoons of melted butter, 2 tablespoons of vinegar or lemon juice, and heat in a double boiler; when it begins to thicken remove from the fire and stir in 1 well-beaten egg. Chop the whites of the boiled eggs, and put with them 2 teaspoons of chopped parsley, and decorate the centre of each broiled tomato with this before serving.

CREAMED TOMATOES

Take solid, medium-sized tomatoes, and, having cut a circular piece out of the stem-end, scoop out most of the inside, and fill with parboiled celery cut in half-inch lengths, mixed with an equal quantity of canned peas, and dampened with white sauce; heap 1 teaspoon of peas on the top of each tomato, and bake for twenty minutes or more, and serve with highly seasoned white sauce poured over each.

BAKED TOMATOES WITH MUSHROOMS

Wash good solid tomatoes and carefully cut out the inside; dredge with pepper and salt and fill the tomato with sauté mushrooms, using either fresh or canned ones, chopped and fried in butter. Bake for about twenty minutes, or until heated through but not broken.

TOMATOES WITH NUT FORCE-MEAT

Slice the stem-end from 6 large, solid tomatoes, scoop out the inside, and fill with a force-meat made of one cup of crumbs, ½ cup of chopped nuts, 1 teaspoon of salt, 1 saltspoon of pepper, 1 tablespoon of melted butter, ½ tablespoon of grated onion, and 1 egg. Replace the tops on the tomatoes and bake them for about twenty minutes, watching that the skins do not break, as they will do in a too hot oven.

TOMATOES STUFFED WITH EGG AND PEPPERS

Cut the inside from solid, large tomatoes, and refill with a mixture of equal parts of chopped hard-boiled eggs and chopped sweet green peppers (or use pimentos) well moistened with melted butter and onion juice, and seasoned with salt. Put in a baking dish, cover, and let bake for twenty minutes in a moderate oven.

BAKED TOMATOES WITH GREEN PEPPERS

Scoop out the inside from solid tomatoes, and refill with the tomato meat which has been cut out of the centre and chopped with sweet green peppers, using 1 teaspoon of peppers to each tomato, and 1 teaspoon of cracker crumbs or boiled rice; season with pepper and salt, and place ¼ teaspoon of butter in each tomato before laying the top on; then bake in a moderate oven about twenty minutes.

TOMATOES FILLED WITH EGG

Select very large solid tomatoes, and with a small, sharp knife cut a round piece out of the stem-end, then cut out a large enough space from the inside to hold a small egg, and arrange in a shallow pan. Sprinkle with salt and pepper, add ½ teaspoon of grated onion, and set in a hot oven for five or six minutes. Remove, and break into each tomato the yolk of 1 egg and as much of the white as it will hold without running over the edge. Sprinkle with salt, pepper, and a little chopped parsley, and replace in the oven, letting them cook slowly fifteen minutes until the egg is set. Remove to individual plates for serving, taking care to not break the tomato. Garnish with cress or parsley.

Tomatoes may be stuffed in a great variety of ways,—with fillings of fried cucumber, tomato, and chopped onions, or bread dressing with sage, etc.

TOMATOES STUFFED WITH SPINACH

Cut an opening in the top of large, solid tomatoes, and scoop out some of the inside with a spoon, fill with "German spinach," and place in a hot oven for about twenty minutes; upon removing from the oven cover each with a slice of hard-boiled egg, or use the white rim filled with riced yolks. Serve alone or as a garnish for another vegetable.

TOMATOES STUFFED WITH MACARONI

Scoop the inside from 6 large, solid tomatoes and use it with 1 bay leaf and some melted butter to make a tomato sauce. Into this stir ½ cup of boiled macaroni (spaghetti or rice may also be used), and, after seasoning well with salt and pepper, fill the tomatoes with the macaroni, putting 1 teaspoon of grated cheese on the top of each. Bake in a moderate oven for about twenty minutes or less, and garnish with watercress or parsley.

AMERICAN RAREBIT

Put a little water and 1 large tablespoon of butter in a frying pan, and when melted add 1 large Spanish onion or 3 ordinary onions chopped fine, and let simmer slowly ten minutes. Strain the juice from a can of tomatoes, and put the tomatoes in a double boiler; when they are heated through scrape the onions into the tomatoes, and let them all cook together for half an hour; season highly with salt and pepper, and just before serving add 2 or 3 well-beaten eggs, and let stand for a few minutes until somewhat thickened; serve on toast. If the flavour of onions is liked, a larger quantity of chopped onion may be used; and to increase the quantity, 3 or 4 more eggs may be added to this rule without other changes. For chafing-dish prepare in advance to the point where the eggs are added, and add these after reheating in the chafing-dish.

TOMATOES AND ONION

Proceed as in the preceding recipe without adding the eggs.

TOMATOES CASINO

Select large, solid tomatoes, and without cutting them let them boil for fifteen minutes; then slip off the skins, halve them, and lay each piece, cut-side down, on a round of toast the same size as the tomato. Cover the top with warm Hollandaise, Bernaise, or Maître d'hôtel sauce, and in the centre lay a slice of truffle; garnish with watercress.

TOMATOES INDIENNE

Halve large, solid tomatoes, and arrange them in a shallow pan, cut-side up. Dredge with salt and pepper, and spread with curry powder and some onion juice. Put in the oven for ten minutes, or under the gas burners of the oven in a gas stove. Do not let the tomatoes soften, and serve at once to prevent this. Use alone or as a garnish to rice.

TOMATOES WITH EGGS

Strain 1 can of tomatoes and put them in a saucepan; stir well, and season with pepper and salt and 1 tablespoon of butter, and, after they have cooked fifteen or twenty minutes, stir in 3 or 4 well-beaten eggs and serve on toast after two or three minutes' further cooking.

CURRIED TOMATOES

Cut a thin slice from the stem-end of large, solid tomatoes, and scoop out some of the inside. Fill with boiled rice to which is added the tomato removed from the inside and a little curry powder (½ teaspoon to 1 cup of rice is a moderate amount). Season the mixture well with salt, replace the top, and bake fifteen minutes. The curry powder can be omitted from the filling and the tomatoes served with curry sauce if preferred.

SAVOURY TOMATOES

Cut in half rather large, solid tomatoes, allowing 2 halves for each person to be served, and set them, cut-side up, in a shallow tin; press capers into the spaces, then dredge heavily with celery salt, sprinkle with salt and pepper, and set under the flame of a gas oven until the tops are blackened. The flame should be hot so that this may happen as quickly as possible in order that the tomatoes may not become softened by the heat; to this end it is also necessary to leave the door of the broiling compartment open.

TOMATOES CREOLE

Cut in half, crosswise, 5 or 6 solid tomatoes, and set them, cut halves upwards, in a buttered pan. Chop 1 or 2 sweet green peppers, mix with them 1 teaspoon of chopped onion, and sprinkle this over the tomatoes; place a small piece of butter on each half, and sprinkle with salt and paprika. Let bake about twenty minutes, then remove to rounds of toast, or nests of boiled rice, and pour over them white sauce.

TOMATO LOAF

Strain the juice from 1 can of tomatoes through a sieve fine enough to stop all the seeds, and put in an enamelled saucepan to boil; season well with salt and pepper, and when it boils pour it onto enough gelatine dissolved in water to stiffen it. The amount of gelatine cannot be given, as the various vegetable gelatines, arrowroot, etc., vary in thickening power. Instructions as to the proper amount for each pint of liquid will come with every package. Set the jelly aside to cool, and arrange slices of hard-boiled egg on the bottom of custard cups or small plain moulds, and encircle these with slices of stuffed olive, pickled walnut, or truffles, or mushrooms. When the jelly is somewhat cooled, and so thick enough to hold down these garnishings when poured onto them, half fill the cups with it. Serve when set and ice-cold, turned out on lettuce leaves.

TOMATOES AND HOMINY

Take 2 cups of cold boiled hominy and 2 cups of boiled tomatoes, put them in a saucepan with 1 tablespoon of butter, season generously with salt and pepper, and serve in a deep dish when thoroughly heated through, or put into a buttered baking dish with crumbs on the top (and a little grated cheese if liked); brown before serving.

STEWED TURNIPS

Peel and wash turnips and cut them in eighths lengthwise, or in dice, and put them in boiling milk and water which covers them. Let them cook slowly for half an hour uncovered, then lift them out and place on a hot dish at the side of the stove. Make a sauce with 1½ cups of the stock in which they cooked, into which beat the yolk of 1 egg and ½ teaspoon of lemon juice; season this with pepper and salt and pour over the turnips. Instead of this, ordinary white sauce may be made of the turnip stock.

MASHED TURNIPS

Peel and quarter 2 good-sized turnips, cover them with boiling water, and let cook until tender, which should be in from half an hour to three quarters; drain them in a colander, and press gently with a wire potato-masher to remove as much water as possible, then mash them and beat them well, stirring in 2 tablespoons of butter, 1 teaspoon of salt, and 1 saltspoon of pepper.

MASHED TURNIPS AND POTATO

Prepare turnips as for mashed turnips, and mash with them an equal quantity of boiled potatoes; add butter, pepper, and salt, and beat up very light before serving.

TURNIPS AU GRATIN

Cut boiled turnips in thin slices, and arrange them in a buttered baking dish in layers one inch deep; sprinkle each layer with melted butter, pepper, salt, and grated cheese. Finish with cheese on the top, and bake for twenty minutes.

RAGOUT OF TURNIPS

Put 2 tablespoons of butter in a saucepan, and when melted add 1 tablespoon of chopped onion and 4 cups of diced turnips, and stir until they begin to brown; season with 1 teaspoon of salt, 1 saltspoon of pepper, 1 teaspoon of sugar, and add slowly 1 cup of vegetable broth or milk into which 1 tablespoon of flour has been made smooth. Let simmer gently for half an hour.

TELTOWER RÜBCHEN

Buy the imported "rübchen," which are the daintiest tiny turnips, and heat them in their own liquor; then drain and serve with Spanish sauce.

PARISIAN TURNIPS

Cut turnips into small rounds with a Parisian potato cutter, and boil them for half an hour or until tender, the time depending largely upon the age of the turnips. Drain, and cover with highly seasoned white sauce, to which 1 tablespoon of chopped parsley has been added.

VEGETABLE COMBINATIONS

CHOP SUEY

Put 1 cup of onions, fried until brown, 1 cup of celery cut in two-inch pieces and then shredded and stewed in vegetable stock for half an hour, 1 cup of fried mushrooms, and 2 cups of boiled rice in a saucepan with a cup of thin brown sauce. Let all heat together for ten minutes, and season with salt and pepper.

COLCANNON

This is made by the mixture of two or more vegetables already boiled. Use equal parts of mashed potato and sprouts (or any greens) finely minced, and grated onion if wanted, and add some mashed carrots or turnips or both; season with salt and pepper. Mix 2 eggs through 4 or 5 cups of vegetables, press into a mould, and boil or steam for half an hour. Turn out to serve, and serve plain or with a brown sauce.

MACEDOINE OF VEGETABLES

Boil 1 small cauliflower and set it aside to drain; then boil 2 cups of diced carrots, drain them when tender, but reserve the stock. Add to the carrots the cauliflower carefully separated into little pieces, 2 cups of boiled peas, or 1 can, 1 cup of cooked or canned flageolets, ½ a cup of carrot stock, 1½ teaspoons of salt, 1 small saltspoon of pepper, and 1 tablespoon of sugar. Let simmer together until heated, and then add 1 chopped onion, 2 bay leaves, 1 tablespoon of butter. If liked, a sauce made of 1 tablespoon of butter and 1 tablespoon of flour thinned with the carrot stock and highly seasoned can be strained over the vegetables before serving.

CANNED MACEDOINE OF VEGETABLES

Delicious combinations of peas, shaped carrots, flageolets, etc., can be had in bottles. Drain them, and put in a saucepan with 1 tablespoon of butter and some pepper and salt. When hot serve or add ½ cup of cream. Serve to garnish, or alone, or use to fill peppers, or tomatoes, or patties.

VEGETABLE CHOWDER

Pare and slice in rather thick slices, enough potatoes to make 4 cups, and prepare the same amount of shredded cabbage, and sliced onions. Put 2 tablespoons of butter in a saucepan, and when melted add the onions, and cook them for ten minutes. Butter a large casserole, arrange over the bottom a layer of sliced potato, then a layer of cabbage, then one of onions, seasoning each with pepper and salt, and sprinkling with chopped hard-boiled egg, and so fill the dish. Pour 2 cups of milk, into which 1 tablespoon of flour has been made smooth, over the chowder, set the dish in a shallow pan of water, and bake slowly for one hour. If the milk cooks away add a little more during the cooking. The same dish can be made in a kettle, in which case halve the potatoes and cook for three quarters of an hour.

VEGETABLE PIE (ST. GEORGE'S HOUSE)

Boil enough carrots, turnips, and large white haricot beans to make a ½ cup of each when chopped or sliced after cooling, and enough potatoes to make a scant cup when sliced. Slice enough Bermuda onions to make ½ cup, and fry in butter until golden brown; then mix the onions and prepared vegetables, and add to them ¼ cup each of canned peas, green beans, and tomatoes. Season well with salt and pepper, stir in 1 teaspoon of chopped parsley, dampen with the water in which the haricot beans cooked, heap into a deep baking dish, cover with a good crust, and bake until slightly browned.

VEGETABLE HASH

Chop separately 5 medium-sized potatoes, 2 sweet green peppers (carefully seeded), 5 fresh tomatoes, 1 cup of boiled beets (½ a can), and 2 raw onions.

Put 2 tablespoons of butter in a frying pan, and when melted add the chopped onions, and let simmer slowly for five minutes, then add the tomatoes and let simmer another five minutes, then put in the potatoes, the peppers, and the beets. Dredge well with salt and pepper, and, stirring occasionally, let all cook slowly until the juices are nearly absorbed; then let the hash brown on the bottom, and turn out with the brown on top. Garnish with squares of toast.

VEGETABLE STEW

Put 4 tablespoons of butter in a large saucepan, and when melted add to it ½ cup of sliced onions, ½ cup of diced carrots, 1 cup of shredded celery, and ¼ cup of turnips cut in oblong pieces, and toss them in the butter for fifteen minutes; then pour over them 6 cups of cold vegetable broth or water, add 1 teaspoon of salt, 2 bay leaves, 6 small onions halved, 4 carrots cut in quarters, 6 small squares of turnip, and let simmer slowly for half an hour; then add 5 potatoes cut in half, and let cook for half an hour more, and add more vegetable broth to keep the vegetables covered. Make dumplings, and drop into the boiling stew, cover tightly, and cook ten minutes more; season well with salt and pepper, and serve with enough of the stock, thickened with a little flour and butter, to cover.

VEGETABLE CASSEROLE

In order that this dish should taste and appear at its best, it should be cooked and served in an Italian casserole dish from eight to ten inches in diameter. Peel 8 medium-sized onions, and take the layers off until a centre about three quarters of an inch in diameter is left; toss the centres in hot butter until browned, and chop the outside. Cut 3 medium-sized sweet green peppers in half, lengthwise, and fill each half liberally with a mixture of bread crumbs, chopped tomato, chopped onion, and salt and pepper. Stuff 6 solid, medium-sized tomatoes in any of the ways described under stuffed tomatoes. Put 2 tablespoons of butter in a saucepan, and when melted add to it 2 tablespoons of chopped onions; fry these for ten minutes, then stir in 2 tablespoons of flour, and use vegetable stock or milk, 2 cups of either, to make a sauce; add 1 bay leaf, and enough soup-browning to make a rich colour. Put the stuffed peppers in a casserole dish with the glazed onion hearts and the sauce, cover, and let cook for ten minutes; then arrange the stuffed tomatoes in the casserole, distribute among them ½ can of button mushrooms, halved, ½ can of flageolets or peas, and leave the cover off the dish, letting it cook for fifteen minutes very slowly. This casserole can be varied in many ways, using different filling for the peppers and tomatoes, and either truffles, string beans, or fresh mushrooms in the sauce, which should not be too thick.

VEGETABLE RAGOUT

Prepare for boiling what will make 3 cups of turnip when cut in inch squares, 1½ cups of potatoes, and 1½ cups of carrots. Put the carrots into slightly salted and sweetened water, let boil for ten minutes, then add the turnips and potato, and cook for ten minutes more. Put 2 tablespoons of butter in a saucepan, and when melted add 2 tablespoons of chopped onion, and fry until slightly browned; then add 2 tablespoons of flour, stir until smooth, and pour slowly into this 2 cups of the stock in which the vegetables cooked; then add 2 teaspoons of sugar, 1 teaspoon of salt, ½ teaspoon of pepper; and the diced vegetables; cover, and let simmer slowly for half an hour, then add 1 tablespoon of chopped parsley, and serve.

BORDEAUX PIE

Slice enough Spanish onions to fill a cup ¼ full, and fry them in butter until slightly browned. Boil carrots to equal ½ cup when diced, potatoes enough to fill a cup ¾ full, and peel 2 cups of mushrooms, and toss them in a little butter in a frying pan over a moderate fire for ten minutes; hard boil 4 eggs, and make 1 cup of white sauce. Cut the vegetables in small pieces, slice the eggs, add ¼ cup of canned peas (or fresh boiled ones), 1 teaspoon of chopped parsley, salt and pepper well, put in a little grated nutmeg and 1 teaspoon of lemon juice, and mix all carefully with the white sauce. Line a large baking dish (or small individual ones) with thin crust, fill with the mixture, cover the top with crust, and bake until slightly browned.

NEW ORLEANS STEW

Slice 3 onions, and fry them in 1 large tablespoon of butter for five minutes; then add to them 3 chopped sweet green peppers, stir well, and let cook together another five minutes; then scrape the contents of the frying pan into a double boiler, add the corn cut from 3 ears of sweet corn (or ½ can of corn), and 3 sliced tomatoes, 1 cup of water, 1 teaspoon of salt, 1 teaspoon of sugar, and let all cook together for one hour; season afresh before serving.

INDIAN CURRY

Put 2 tablespoons of butter in a frying pan, and add to it when melted 2 onions chopped fine, and let cook very slowly for fifteen minutes. Mix 1 tablespoon of curry powder, 1 tablespoon of sour apple, or tamarind-chutney chopped fine, 1 teaspoon of salt, and enough vegetable stock to make a paste. When the onions are browned add this paste, and after stirring well put in 1 cup of boiled haricot beans, 1 cup of halved boiled chestnuts, and 1 can of halved button mushrooms, and let all simmer together for ten minutes. Have ready some stock made by putting 2 tablespoons of desiccated cocoanut into a bowl and pouring over it 1 cup of boiling water, and use this to dampen the cooking vegetables; then add 1 cup of vegetable broth, and let cook ten minutes more. We westerners are fond of this served in this way with chutney, but in India they press it through a strainer and serve it as a purée, adding to it 2 well-beaten eggs. Encircle with rice in serving.

CURRY OF LENTILS

Soak 2 or 3 cups of German or Egyptian lentils for two or three hours; drain them, and put them in boiling water, and let them cook for three quarters of an hour or until tender but not broken. Salt well when they have been cooking a short time, and when done drain them, sprinkle with salt, and heap in a pyramid on a round flat dish; garnish with 3 hard-boiled eggs cut in half, encircle with boiled rice, and pour curry sauce over the lentils only. Serve extra sauce in a sauce-boat and Indian chutney.

CURRY OF SUCCOTASH

Heat 1 can of Lima beans and 1 can of sweet corn, and when hot drain, and heap on a flat dish; cover with curry sauce, and serve with potato croquettes and Indian chutney.

CREOLE CURRY

Boil 1 cup of rice, and while it is cooking put 2 cups of okra, 2 cups of tomato, and 2 small onions cut in halves, and 1 teaspoon of butter in a double boiler, and when hot add 1 cup of hot water, into which has been dissolved 1 heaping teaspoon of curry powder, and let all cook together for half an hour; remove the onions, add the rice, season generously with salt, and serve with Indian chutney.

VARIOUS VEGETABLE CURRIES

Almost any vegetable makes a good curry,—flageolets, carrots and peas, button mushrooms, etc., and either boiled rice or rice croquettes should be served. A garnish of Spanish pimentos looks well, and the curry sauce should be plentiful. Hard-boiled eggs halved are always nice with curry, and Indian chutney should be served with it.

NUT DISHES

ITALIAN CHESTNUTS

Chestnuts can be cooked either by roasting or by boiling. If roasted, the thin brown that clings to the nut is removed with the outer shell; if boiled, the inner skin often has to be removed with some trouble. Roast chestnuts by putting them in a hot oven for eight or ten minutes, then use a small, sharp knife and peel them from the point down.

To boil chestnuts put them, in their shells, in cold water and let them cook for five or six minutes after the water starts boiling, or put them in boiling water for ten or twelve minutes. Peel carefully, and serve after roasting or boiling with brown sauce or mushroom sauce, plain or in cases.

CHESTNUT PURÉE

Roast or boil 6 cups of Italian chestnuts, remove the shell and inner skin and chop them fine or put them through a vegetable mill. Put them in a double boiler with milk enough to cover them and let them cook slowly for fifteen or twenty minutes, or until the milk is all absorbed. Stir frequently, add 1 tablespoon of butter, 1 tablespoon of cream, plenty of salt and a little pepper. The purée should be the consistency of mashed potato.

PEANUT PURÉE

Shell 3 or 4 cups of peanuts, remove the inner skin, and put through a vegetable mill. Put in a double boiler with milk to cover them, season with salt, and let cook gently half an hour, or until tender. Stir frequently, and serve when the milk is absorbed and the peanut purée is the consistency of mashed potato. A tablespoon of whipped cream is an improvement if added during the last moments of cooking.

MICHAELMAS LOAF

Mix 1 cup of finely ground walnuts (or other nuts), 1 cup of finely ground roasted peanuts, 1 teaspoon of salt, 1 saltspoon of pepper, 2½ cups of fine bread crumbs, 1 tablespoon of mixed sweet herbs (thyme, sage, and summer savory), and 1 large onion or 2 small ones chopped fine. When well blended bind together with 2 eggs which have been slightly beaten, mould with the hands into a loaf, place in a well buttered roasting tin, and let it cook for ten minutes in a moderately hot oven; then add 1 tablespoon of butter and 1 cup of hot water, and baste frequently during half an hour's cooking. The loaf should be well browned and carefully removed to a hot platter. Make a brown sauce in the pan in which the loaf cooked, and serve with this and cold apple sauce.

NUT AND FRUIT LOAF

Chop mixed nuts enough to make 2 cups, and add to them 6 bananas chopped fine and ½ teaspoon of salt; mix well together, and press into a plain mould. Stand the mould in a steamer, and let it steam for three hours. Serve ice-cold, sliced, with pickles or catsup.

CHRISTMAS LOAF

Make as in foregoing recipe, omitting the chopped onion and adding another half tablespoon (or even more) of the sweet herbs. Serve with cranberry sauce.

ROAST NUT AND BARLEY LOAF

Make a brown sauce with 2 tablespoons of olive oil, ½ cup of browned flour, and use water or vegetable stock for thinning; chop 1 large onion fine, and fry it in 1 tablespoon of oil or butter, and mix the onion and the sauce with 2 cups of cold boiled pearl barley, 1 cup of finely ground roasted peanuts, 1 cup of fine bread crumbs, 1 teaspoon of salt, and 1 saltspoon of pepper. With the hands mould into a loaf, place in a roasting pan which has been well buttered, and let cook in the oven for ten minutes; then add 1 tablespoon of butter and 1 cup of hot water, and baste every five minutes for half an hour. Make a brown sauce in the same pan, or serve with Caper sauce. Garnish, if brown sauce is used, with English savoury croquettes.

STEAMED NUT AND BARLEY LOAF

Make as in the foregoing recipe, but pack into a mould, set this in boiling water, and let it steam for an hour and a half or two hours. Let cool in the mould, and turn out to serve cold, or to slice, or to use for nut hash.

A brick-shaped mould will be made by any tinsmith to order, or the large sizes of baking-powder tins can be used to steam loaf.

ROASTED NUT LOAF WITH HOMINY

Grind 2 cups of nuts,—pecans, walnuts, roasted peanuts, etc., or use peanuts only,—and mix with them 2 cups of cold boiled hominy, ½ cup of bread crumbs, 3 hard-boiled eggs chopped fine, 1 tablespoon of chopped parsley, 1 tablespoon of grated onion, and 1 raw egg. Form into 1 large roll, or several smaller ones, put in a buttered tin, and let bake in a quick oven for half an hour; baste with a little butter and water a few times. Garnish with slices of lemon, and serve with brown sauce. This loaf may be steamed as directed for barley loaf and used hot, cold, or in hash.

FOUNDATION LOAF

This loaf can be made and kept in readiness for use, as it will remain fresh for several days if it is left in the covered mould in which it cooked and is kept in a cool place. Put 2 cups of water in a saucepan, and when the water boils stir into it 1 cup of a finely ground cereal, preferably gluten flour or meal, or Scotch oatmeal, and stir until thick; then add 2 teaspoons of salt, ½ teaspoon of pepper, 1 tablespoon of butter, and 1 cup of shelled peanuts which have been put through a vegetable grinder twice. Pack the mixture into a loaf-shaped mould, or large round tin with a tight-fitting lid, almost immerse it in water, and let it steam for two hours. Use when cold, either for nut hash or croquettes, or with an equal amount of bread crumbs and the seasoning to make Michaelmas or Christmas loaf.

NUT HASH

Use cold steamed nut loaf and the same amount of cold boiled potatoes. Chop the potatoes and the loaf separately, and add to them, after mixing, ¼ as much chopped onion. Turn into a frying pan which contains melted butter well covering the bottom, dredge with salt and pepper, and stir frequently with a knife during the first ten minutes' slow cooking; then let the hash brown on the bottom, shaking the pan vigorously from time to time, season afresh, and turn out with the browned portion on top. One or 2 chopped green peppers can be added to the hash, if the flavour is liked.

RICE, MACARONI, Etc.

BOILED RICE

Wash 1 cup of rice by letting water run through it in a sieve, and put it in a large double boiler, the top of which contains plenty of water at boiling point; add 1 teaspoon of salt, and let it boil, tightly covered, for twenty-five minutes; pour off the water then from the rice, still holding the cover on, and again place it over the boiler, and let the rice steam for another twenty minutes, when it will be found that each grain is separate, as it should be. Use a fork to scrape it lightly into the serving dish.

BAKED RICE

Let ½ cup of rice soak for several hours in 2 cups of warm water. Drain and put in a baking dish, and cover with 3 cups of milk containing ½ a teaspoon of salt. Cover the dish, and let bake slowly for an hour or until the milk is absorbed and the separate grains of rice are soft.

INDIAN RICE

Put 1 tablespoon of butter into a double boiler, and when melted add 1 onion chopped fine, the juice from 1 can of tomatoes, 6 tablespoons of rice, 1 teaspoon of curry powder, some salt and pepper. Cover and let cook together for three quarters of an hour.

SPANISH RICE

Put 2 tablespoons of butter in a saucepan, and when melted add ½ cup of rice, and stir it for fifteen minutes; then add 1 chopped onion, 1 chopped tomato, and 1 clove of garlic, cover with hot water or vegetable stock, and season highly with salt and pepper; stir well, then cover, and let the rice cook slowly for forty minutes.

RICE-TOMATO STEW

Take 1 cup of cold boiled rice, and put with it in a saucepan 1 teaspoon of butter, 3 or 4 sliced tomatoes (or a cup of drained canned ones), 1 bay leaf, some celery salt, pepper and salt, and stir well together; let cook slowly for ten minutes, taking care that it does not burn; remove the bay leaf, and serve on thick slices of toast.

FRIED RICE

Press newly boiled rice into an inch-deep pan, cover with a weight, and let it become cold. Cut into two-inch squares, and fry until brown in hot butter. Serve with tomato or curry sauce.

ESCALLOPED RICE

Butter a baking dish, and sprinkle the bottom with a layer of boiled rice, and cover this with slices of hard-boiled eggs; dot well with butter, sprinkle with salt and pepper, then arrange another layer of rice and egg, etc., alternating thus until the dish is filled. Cover the top with bread crumbs, pour over all 2 tablespoons of melted butter, moisten with ½ cup of milk, and bake slowly for twenty minutes.

RICE AND CHEESE

Butter a baking dish well, and sprinkle a half-inch layer of boiled rice on the bottom; season with salt and pepper, and dot well with butter; then arrange a generous layer of grated cheese, and sprinkle this with English mustard mixed with water, then add another layer of rice, and so continue until the dish is well filled, having the rice on top. Pour over all ½ cup of milk, or of the water in which the rice boiled, and let cook slowly in the oven for twenty minutes.

BAKED RICE AND TOMATOES

Butter a baking dish well, and put a layer of rice in the bottom of it, and over this arrange slices of tomatoes; dot well with butter, and season plentifully with pepper and salt and celery salt, then place another layer of rice, and so proceed until the dish is well filled. Pour ½ cup of canned tomato juice over the rice, sprinkle the top with grated cheese, and bake for twenty minutes.

ITALIAN RICE

Put 1 tablespoon of butter in a saucepan, and when melted add to it 2 cups of boiled rice and 1 cup of tomato sauce or tomato chutney; season well with salt and pepper, stir until heated through, and serve plentifully sprinkled with grated cheese.

RICE AU GRATIN

Put 1 cup of milk in a double boiler, when hot add to it 1 tablespoon of flour mixed with 1 tablespoon of butter, 1 teaspoon of grated onion (or a few drops of onion extract), and ½ teaspoon of salt; stir into this 2 cups of boiled rice, let cook for five minutes, then put in a buttered baking dish, with ½ cup of grated cheese on top, dredge this with paprika, sprinkle with bread crumbs, and let brown in the oven.

RICE OMELET

Beat the yolks and whites of 2 eggs separately, and to the yolks add ¼ of a cup of milk, ⅓ of a cup of cold boiled rice, 1 tablespoon of melted butter, some salt and pepper, and finally the stiff whites of the eggs. Put in a buttered omelet pan, and proceed as in making the usual omelet, cooking over a slow fire and shaking the pan vigorously. Sprinkle with salt and a little paprika; when set, turn together; serve with a sauce if desired, and garnish with watercress.

RICE CZARINA

Butter a baking dish, and put an inch-deep layer of boiled rice in the bottom. Over this sprinkle finely chopped fresh or canned tomatoes, season with salt and pepper, and dot well with butter; then place another layer of rice somewhat thinner, and over this spread finely chopped green peppers, and so alternate tomatoes, peppers, and rice until the dish is well filled, having a layer of rice on the top. Garnish this with thin slices of tomato in the centre, and encircle the edge with thinly cut rings from the peppers. Pour 2 tablespoons of melted butter over all, cover lightly with a tin cover, and let cook in a slow oven for twenty minutes; just before serving add 2 more tablespoons of melted butter.

SAVOURY RICE

Butter a baking dish, and half fill it with freshly boiled rice, sprinkle this with salt, pepper, celery salt, and a few drops of Worcestershire Sauce, then dot with mustard mixed with water, and pour ½ cup of tomato sauce over the surface evenly. Fill the dish with the remaining rice, and season again with the same ingredients, adding ½ cup of grated cheese (sage cheese preferably); after pouring on the tomato sauce cover with a thin layer of crumbs and bake fifteen minutes in a slow oven.

UNPOLISHED RICE

Unpolished rice is used extensively in rice-growing countries, and has a quite distinct taste. When it can be obtained it makes a pleasant change, and can be served in any of the ways described for rice.

PEARL BARLEY

Pearl barley should be put in plenty of boiling water and cooked for an hour, then drained, and prepared in any of the ways described for the serving of rice.

AMERICAN MACARONI

Break ¼ of a package of macaroni into two-inch lengths, and drop it into rapidly boiling salted water. Let it boil for twenty-five minutes, then drain, and arrange with alternate layers of grated cheese in a buttered baking dish. Season each layer with pepper and salt, and when the dish is filled pour over all 1 cup of hot milk into which 1 tablespoon of flour and 1 of butter have been made smooth. Cover the top with crumbs and bake twenty minutes or until browned.

Some makers of macaroni recommend putting the macaroni in cold water for fifteen minutes after boiling it, and then reheating it with seasoning, etc.

MACARONI AU GRATIN

Break ¼ of a package of macaroni into two-inch lengths, and put it into 2 quarts of rapidly boiling salted water; let boil rapidly for twenty-five minutes, then drain. Butter a baking dish, and put in it a half-inch layer of the macaroni, sprinkle generously with grated cheese, and season with salt and pepper; then put another layer of macaroni, and proceed as before until the dish is well filled, having macaroni on the top. Dot evenly with butter, and bake about fifteen minutes or until a golden brown.

MACARONI BIANCA

Break half a package of macaroni into two-inch lengths, and drop it slowly into 2 quarts of rapidly boiling salted water; in fifteen minutes pour off all but 1 cup of the water, and add ½ cup of hot milk, stir often with a fork, and let boil until nearly dry or until tender, which will be in ten or fifteen minutes, and lift the macaroni into a strainer the instant it is cooked. Butter a baking dish, and put in it a layer of macaroni, dredge with salt and pepper, then sprinkle lightly with a layer of grated cheese (using 1 cup for the whole dish); dot well with mixed mustard, and sprinkle with Worcestershire sauce. Fill the dish with layers in this way, pour ½ cup of milk over all, and bake fifteen or twenty minutes, or until brown, in a quick oven.

ITALIAN MACARONI

Break ¼ of a pound of macaroni into four-inch lengths, put in boiling salted water, and let it cook for twenty-five minutes. Drain, and put in a saucepan with 1 tablespoon of melted butter and 1½ cups of tomato sauce; season well with salt and pepper, and serve on a hot flat dish with grated cheese plentifully sprinkled over it.

MACARONI WITH TOMATO AND ONION SAUCE

Boil ¼ of a package of macaroni in rapidly boiling salted water for twenty-five minutes, and whilst it is cooking prepare a sauce as follows: Put a large tablespoon of butter in a saucepan, and when melted stir into it 1 minced onion, 1 tablespoon of chopped parsley, and season with salt and pepper. Let cook together for six or seven minutes, then add 1 tablespoon of flour and 1 cup of stewed and strained tomatoes, and stir well together for five minutes. Butter a baking dish, put a layer of macaroni in it, then a layer of sauce, and so on till the dish is well filled, and set in the oven for ten minutes before serving.

BAKED MACARONI ITALIAN

Boil ¼ of a pound of macaroni broken in two-inch lengths for twenty-five minutes, then drain, and put it in a buttered baking dish with 1 cup of tomato sauce; season well with salt and pepper, and put a half-inch layer of grated cheese on the top, and bake for fifteen minutes.

MEXICAN MACARONI

Put 1 tablespoon of butter in a saucepan, and when melted stir into it ½ a can of tomatoes, 1 small sweet green pepper, seeded and chopped fine, 1 large onion chopped fine, and ½ teaspoon of salt. Cover, and let cook very slowly for about forty minutes. Then press through a coarse sieve, and put in a double boiler to keep hot. Boil ¼ of a package of macaroni for twenty-five minutes, drain, and pour over it the hot sauce.

PLAIN MACARONI AND CHEESE

Put ¼ of a package of macaroni into boiling water, and let cook twenty-five minutes; drain, add 1 cup of hot milk, 1 tablespoon of butter, salt, pepper, and paprika; let boil up once, add ½ cup of grated cheese, and let cook five minutes more before serving.

MACARONI RAREBIT

Put in a saucepan 2 tablespoons of butter, and when melted add 1 cup of grated cheese and stir until the cheese is melted, and then add ½ a teaspoon of salt, ½ a teaspoon of mustard, ½ teaspoon of paprika, and 1 tablespoon of flour dissolved in ½ cup of cream (or milk), to which also add 3 slightly beaten eggs; mix all together thoroughly, put in 1 cup of cooked macaroni, and serve with toast.

SPAGHETTI

Spaghetti can be cooked in any of the ways described for macaroni, but real Neapolitan spaghetti is cooked as follows:—Break 1 lb. of spaghetti into 3 or 4 inch lengths, and put in a large saucepan full of highly salted boiling water and let boil for half an hour. At the same time put 1 cup of good olive oil in a frying pan and when hot put in it 2 green peppers, seeded and chopped, and let simmer until they begin to brown, then add 4 to 6 cloves of garlic cut fine, and 4 large tomatoes, peeled, quartered, and thinly sliced. Let cook for about half an hour or until the oil is all absorbed, and stir often. When cooked to the consistency of a thick sauce, sprinkle with salt and paprika; drain the spaghetti thoroughly, mix the sauce through it and serve on a large platter, sprinkling with freshly grated Parmesan cheese.

NOODLES

To make noodles add ½ cup of sifted flour containing ¼ of a teaspoon of salt to 1 large egg which has been slightly beaten. Mix well with a fork, and when stiff enough work with the fingers until the dough becomes very smooth and about the consistency of putty, and then wrap in a cloth and lay aside for half an hour. Sprinkle a bread-board well with flour, and roll the dough out upon this five or six times, rolling it thinner each time; at the last roll it as thin as possible without breaking, then roll it lightly together like a jelly-cake roll, and with a very sharp knife, beginning at one end, cut it into slices about ⅛ of an inch wide if to be used for soup, and ⅜ of an inch wide if to be used with a sauce. With the fingers shake these ribbons until they are separated, and let them dry for about half an hour.

Cut about ⅛ of the noodles very fine, and when dried, drop these in hot oil and fry until crisp and brown; serve these sprinkled over the boiled noodles.

To boil noodles, drop them in rapidly boiling salted water, cover them, and let them boil for twenty minutes, and then drain thoroughly.

Boiled noodles are delicious served with any brown sauce or tomato sauce, and can be used as directed for macaroni or spaghetti.

Very good noodles can be bought already made.

GERMAN NOODLES

Put 2 cups of dried noodles into boiling salted water, let them cook rapidly for twenty minutes, drain, and put in a saucepan with 1 tablespoon of butter and 1 cup of brown sauce, to which has been added 1 tablespoon of reduced vinegar and a few capers if liked. Serve when thoroughly heated through, and add a little salt and pepper when in the dish.

ITALIAN NOODLES

Put 2 cups of dried noodles into boiling salted water, let cook twenty minutes, drain, and put in a saucepan with 1 tablespoon of butter and 1 cup of tomato sauce or chutney. Season with pepper and salt, and serve on a hot dish, with the top well sprinkled with grated cheese.

CROQUETTES

BEAN CROQUETTES

Wash 2 cups of dried beans, then soak them in water for twelve hours or more, and cook in the same water about an hour or until tender; strain off the water, press through a sieve, and add 1 teaspoon of salt, 1 saltspoon of pepper, 1 tablespoon of butter. Stir well together, shape into croquettes, dip in beaten egg and crumbs, and fry in deep vegetable fat. Serve with tomato or horse-radish sauce.

CHEESE CROQUETTES

Beat the white of 1 egg very stiff, and stir into it 1 cup of fine bread crumbs, 1 cup of grated cheese, ½ teaspoon of salt, and 1 saltspoon of paprika. Shape into balls or croquette forms, then roll in the beaten yolk of egg and crumbs, put in a frying basket, and fry in boiling vegetable fat until a golden brown. Lay on brown paper in the oven for three minutes, then arrange in a heap on a paper doily, dust with grated cheese, and garnish with watercress or parsley.

SWISS CHEESE CROQUETTES

Melt 3 tablespoons of butter, add a few drops of onion juice, ¼ cup of flour, ½ cup of milk, the yolks of 2 eggs, 1 cup of grated American cheese, and ½ cup of Swiss cheese cut into small pieces. Let cook in a double boiler until the cheese is melted, then season with salt and cayenne; let cool, then shape into croquettes, roll in crumbs, and fry in deep fat.

CHESTNUT CROQUETTES

Peel, blanch, and chop fine enough Italian chestnuts to make 2 cups, and boil them in water or milk to cover them for three quarters of an hour or until they are tender and the milk absorbed; let cool somewhat, then add 1 cup of bread crumbs, and 1 beaten egg, and ½ teaspoon of salt. Shape into croquettes, roll in egg and crumbs, and fry in deep fat. Serve with mushroom sauce or as a garnish.

EGG CROQUETTES

Hard boil 10 or 12 eggs, add to them 1 tablespoon of chopped parsley, chop very fine, and season highly; then moisten with milk or cream. Mould into shape, roll in egg and crumbs, and fry in hot fat. Serve as a garnish to rice or tomatoes, or as a separate dish alone, or with curry sauce, horse-radish sauce, tomato sauce, or devilled sauce.

FARINA CROQUETTES

Put 2 cups of milk in a double boiler, and when hot add 1 cup of farina and some salt. Cook until well thickened, and then whip vigorously into it 1 beaten egg. Let cool, mould into croquettes, dip in crumbs, and fry in hot fat. Serve with savoury sauce or with jelly melted to the consistency of cream.

HOMINY CROQUETTES

Put 1 pint of cooked hominy into a saucepan, add 2 tablespoons of cream or milk, and stir over the fire until hot, then remove from the fire and season with salt; add the yolks of 2 eggs lightly beaten, shape into croquettes, roll in crumbs, and fry until nicely browned. Serve with some savoury sauce or as a garnish to scrambled or fried eggs.

LENTIL CROQUETTES

Put 1 cup of well-washed lentils into 3 cups of water or vegetable broth when at boiling point, and let them cook slowly for an hour or until tender, strain them, and mash them in water, and let them cool.

Put 1 tablespoon of butter in a saucepan, and when melted add 1 finely chopped onion, and let cook for ten minutes; add this to the lentils, with 2 slices of bread which have been well soaked in milk, 2 beaten eggs, and enough fine bread crumbs to make the mixture thick enough to form into croquettes. Season highly with salt and pepper, shape into form, roll in egg, and then in crumbs, put in a frying basket, and fry in deep fat. Serve with horse-radish or onion sauce.

Lentil croquettes may also be served with caper sauce, and each croquette garnished with a slice of seeded lemon.

MACARONI CROQUETTES

Have ready a kettle of salted boiling water, then shake into it ½ cup of macaroni, and let boil briskly for half an hour; then drain, and cut into small pieces. While the macaroni is cooking, make a sauce of 1 cup of hot milk to which is added 1 tablespoon of butter and 2 tablespoons of flour rubbed together, to which add, when thickened, the yolks of 2 eggs well beaten, 1 teaspoon of salt, 1 saltspoon of pepper, and the chopped macaroni (the sauce must not cook after the eggs are added). Turn out to cool, and when cold form into pyramid-shaped croquettes, roll in egg and crumbs, and fry in deep fat. Serve with tomato sauce and a little sprinkling of grated cheese.

ITALIAN CROQUETTES

Put 1 tablespoon of butter in a saucepan, and when melted add 1 finely chopped onion, let cook slowly for five minutes, then add 2 cups of boiled macaroni, 1 cup of milk, cover, and stirring frequently let simmer slowly for half an hour or until the milk is absorbed; add 1 cup of drained canned tomatoes, or 2 or 3 chopped fresh ones, and 1 tablespoon of grated cheese, 1 teaspoon of mixed mustard, 1 tablespoon of highly flavoured catsup, salt and pepper. Cook for ten minutes more, then add ½ cup of bread crumbs and 2 teaspoons of chopped parsley. Turn into a bowl, and when somewhat cooled add 1 beaten egg and stir it well through the mixture. When cool and firm form into shapes, brush with egg, roll in crumbs, and fry a golden brown in deep fat. Serve plain or with tomato or curry sauce.

TOMATO CROQUETTES

Take ¾ of a cup of stewed tomatoes without any juice, put in a saucepan over the fire, and stir into them 1 tablespoon of butter, 1 cup of mashed potatoes, ½ cup of grated bread crumbs, and some salt and pepper. Mix well together, and then add 1 lightly beaten egg. Remove from the fire, turn into a deep plate, and when cold form into croquettes; dip each in egg and bread crumbs, fry until brown, and serve with a savoury sauce.

DRIED PEA CROQUETTES

Put 1 cup of dried peas in cold water or broth, let cook for 1½ hours or until tender, then strain and mash. Add to them 1 finely minced onion which has been fried ten minutes in 1 tablespoon of butter, salt, pepper, 2 tablespoons of flour, 2 eggs, and bread crumbs to make stiff enough to shape into croquettes or flat cakes. Roll in crumbs, and fry golden brown in deep fat. Serve with onion or tomato or mint sauce.

NUT CROQUETTES WITH POTATO

Chop or grind 2 cups of mixed nuts, and mix with them 2 cups of mashed potatoes, 1 teaspoon of grated onion, 1 teaspoon of salt, 1 dash of nutmeg, and 2 yolks of raw eggs. Shape into croquettes, dip in egg, and crumbs, and fry in hot, deep vegetable fat.

NUT CROQUETTES WITH SALSIFY

Use ½ cup each of ground pecans and walnuts, and with them mix 2 cups of boiled mashed salsify, 1 teaspoon of salt, 1 tablespoon of grated onion, 1 tablespoon of chopped parsley, 2 tablespoons of bread crumbs, form into croquettes, roll in egg and crumbs and fry in deep fat. Serve with tomato chutney.

NUT CROQUETTES WITH COCOANUT

Grind 1 cup of any sort of nuts, and add to them 2 cups of bread crumbs, ½ cup of grated cocoanut, 4 tablespoons of peanut butter, ½ teaspoon of celery seed, 1 teaspoon of salt, and 1 egg, well beaten. Mix well, and form into croquettes or balls, dip in egg and crumbs, and fry in deep vegetable fat.

Nut croquettes can be made of the mixtures given for nut loaf, rolled in egg and crumbs and fried.

POTATO CROQUETTES

Take 2 cups of mashed potatoes and stir into them 2 lightly beaten eggs, ½ teaspoon of salt, and a little paprika, and 1 tablespoon of chopped chives or parsley; form into croquettes or rolls, roll in egg and fine crumbs, and fry in deep fat.

POTATO CROQUETTES WITH CHEESE

To 2 cups of cold mashed potatoes add the beaten yolk of 1 egg, 1 tablespoon of grated cheese, 1 tablespoon of milk or cream, and a few drops of onion extract; season with pepper and salt, form into shapes and fry in deep fat.

SAVOURY POTATO CROQUETTES

To 2 cups of cold mashed potatoes add 1 beaten egg, 1 chopped onion, 1 tablespoon of chopped parsley, 1 tablespoon of mixed sweet herbs, and 1 tablespoon of cream. Shape, roll in egg and fine crumbs, and fry in deep fat.

MASHED POTATO CROQUETTES WITH PEAS

To 2 cups of cold mashed potatoes add 1 egg, pepper and salt, and form into flat, small cakes; in the centre of each put 1 teaspoon of canned peas, then lap the potato mixture over these, and form into balls. Dip in egg and crumbs and fry in deep fat.

CREOLE POTATO CROQUETTES

To 2 cups of mashed potatoes add 1 beaten egg, pepper and salt, and 2 tablespoons of chopped green peppers (or chopped red pimentos) which have been fried in butter for ten minutes; shape, roll in egg and crumbs, and fry in deep fat.

SWEET POTATO CROQUETTES

To 2 cups of mashed sweet potato add 1 beaten egg, pepper and salt; shape and roll in egg and crumbs, and fry in deep fat.

SWEETENED RICE CROQUETTES

Soak 1 cup of rice three hours in warm water, then drain and put into a double boiler with 1 pint of boiling milk, and let cook for half an hour; then add 1 tablespoon of sugar, 1 tablespoon of melted butter, and ½ teaspoon of salt, and let simmer ten minutes more. Let cool somewhat, and then stir in slowly 3 eggs, which have been beaten to a froth, and stir until it thickens; then add the grated peel of 1 lemon, and turn out upon a dish to cool. When cold and quite stiff form into balls or oval croquettes, dip in very fine cracker crumbs, and fry in deep fat. Serve alone with sauce or as a garnish.

CAROLINA CROQUETTES

Boil eggs ten minutes, remove the shells, press the yolks through a sieve or potato-ricer, chop the whites fine, and mix with the same amount of boiled rice; dampen with a little melted butter, season with pepper and salt, form into balls, roll in egg and crumbs, and fry in deep fat. When a golden brown drain and serve with some savoury hot sauce, or as a garnish to curry.

PLAIN RICE CROQUETTES

Mix together 2 cups of cold boiled rice, ½ teaspoon of salt, and 1 tablespoon of melted butter, 1 tablespoon of flour, and 1 beaten egg. Form into balls, roll in flour, and fry in deep fat. Serve while crisp.

PINK RICE CROQUETTES

Make croquettes as above, but omit the sugar and add ¼ teaspoon of paprika and 2 tablespoons of tomato catsup to the rice before frying.

CURRIED RICE CROQUETTES

Put ¾ of a cup of milk in a saucepan with butter the size of an egg and let it boil; then stir into it 1 cup of rice that has boiled twenty minutes in salted water. Add 1 small teaspoon of curry powder, a few drops of onion juice, and salt to taste. When the milk boils remove from the fire and add a beaten egg to it, stirring vigorously. Let cool, shape into croquettes, and fry in hot fat. Serve apple sauce or onion sauce with these croquettes.

ENGLISH SAVOURY CROQUETTES

To each cup of fine bread crumbs use 1 tablespoon of mixed sweet herbs and 1 teaspoon of minced onions and bind all together with 1 egg, slightly beaten. Season with ½ teaspoon of salt, 1 scant saltspoon of pepper, ½ teaspoon of celery salt, form into balls, roll in egg, and then in crumbs, and fry in deep fat until golden brown. Serve with a brown sauce or as a garnish to nut loaf.

MIXED VEGETABLE CROQUETTES

Boil separately ten carrots and 3 turnips and 5 potatoes and chop fine; then mash, and add to them 1 tablespoon of butter and 3 tablespoons of hot milk. Put 1 tablespoon of butter in a frying pan, and when melted cook slowly in it for ten minutes, or until beginning to brown, 1 large onion chopped fine. Add this to the mashed vegetables, also 1 tablespoon of chopped parsley, and season with salt and pepper. When cool form them into croquettes or flat cakes, and dip in egg, and then in fine crumbs, and fry. If croquettes are made fry in deep, hot fat; if cakes are made they can be fried in a frying pan like pancakes, and browned on one side, then on the other. Serve plain, or as a garnish to other vegetables, or with Spanish sauce.

Any of the mixtures for croquettes can be moulded into flat cakes and fried until browned in butter on a griddle or in a shallow frying pan.

TIMBALES AND PATTIES

EGG TIMBALES

Into 1 cup of milk rub 1 heaping tablespoon of flour until smoothed, add 1 tablespoon (measured before melting) of butter, the lightly beaten yolks of 4 eggs, ½ teaspoon of salt, 1 saltspoon of pepper, and the same amount of celery salt. Beat the whites of the eggs until very stiff, and stir these into the other ingredients with a fork. Turn into buttered timbale moulds, and set these in a pan containing hot water which almost reaches the top of the moulds. Let bake in a moderate oven for fifteen or twenty minutes or until well set. Turn out on a hot, flat dish and serve with tomato sauce or bread sauce.

SAVOURY EGG TIMBALES

Make the foregoing recipe, but add 1 tablespoon of chopped onion and 1 tablespoon of chopped parsley, or substitute minced shallots, chives, or onion tops.

EGG-TOMATO TIMBALES

Make plain egg timbales, but instead of using milk use 1 cup of tomato juice from canned tomatoes. Add 1 tablespoon of chopped parsley, or chives if desired.

PEA TIMBALES

Take 1½ cups of boiled peas, put them through a ricer, or mash to a pulp, and when cooled add to this 2 lightly beaten eggs, 1 teaspoon of chopped mint, 1 teaspoon of grated onion (or chopped chives), 2 tablespoons of melted butter, ½ teaspoon of salt, and 1 saltspoon of pepper. Fill timbale moulds, set in a pan containing some hot water, and cook in a moderate oven fifteen or twenty minutes or until well set. Turn out and serve with sauce.

CORN TIMBALES

Take 1 cup of canned corn and add to it 4 eggs slightly beaten, ½ teaspoon of salt, a little paprika, ½ teaspoon of onion juice, ½ teaspoon of sugar, and 1¼ cups of milk. Pour into buttered timbale moulds, or a large mould, and set in hot water, and bake in the oven about twenty minutes or until firm. Turn out and garnish with slices of broiled tomatoes.

POTATO AND CHEESE TIMBALES

Take 6 or 7 good-sized potatoes, boil and mash them, and beat into them 4 tablespoons of butter and 2 eggs; then add 1 cup of grated cheese, 1 teaspoon of salt, and some paprika, press into small moulds or cups, and let cook as directed above for about twenty minutes. Turn from the moulds, and serve with a sauce of melted butter to which is added a little grated cheese, paprika, and chopped parsley.

POTATO TIMBALES

Beat 3 eggs (yolks and whites together), add to them ¼ of a cup of cream, then 2 cups of mashed potatoes, 1 teaspoon of grated onion, a little pepper, 1 teaspoon of salt, and some nutmeg; beat together until perfectly smooth, and then press into timbale moulds, the bottoms of which are covered with buttered paper. Stand these in a shallow pan containing boiling water in the oven, and let cook for about twenty minutes. Then loosen the sides with a thin knife, and turn out carefully onto a heated flat dish. Garnish with peas or macedoine vegetables, or use as a garnish.

RICE TIMBALES

To 1 cup of boiled rice add 1 chopped hard-boiled egg, 1 tablespoon of tomato catsup, ½ teaspoon of salt, 1 saltspoon of pepper, 2 tablespoons of melted butter, and 2 well-beaten eggs. Fill well-buttered timbale moulds with this mixture, set them in a pan containing warm water, and bake in a slow oven for twenty minutes, or until well set.

Timbale cases, pastry cases, ramekins, or patties may be filled with any of the following recipes and served as a separate course at luncheon or dinner.

ARTICHOKE PATTIES

Boil Jerusalem artichokes as directed, cut in half-inch cubes, cover with a highly seasoned white sauce, and use to fill patties or cases.

ASPARAGUS PATTIES

Use only the tender ends of white or green canned asparagus, heat in white sauce, and use to fill cases or patties.

CELERY PATTIES

Use celery prepared as in creamed celery, only cut the stalks into inch-long pieces. Fill heated pastry cups or patties with the mixture.

CHESTNUTS IN CASES

Peel 2 cups of Italian chestnuts, and blanch them by pouring boiling water on them and letting them stay in it until the skins remove easily; then cut them in quarters, put them in boiling water, and boil them half an hour or until soft. While they are finishing cooking put 1 tablespoon of butter in a saucepan, and let it cook slowly until a rich dark brown then add to it 1 tablespoon of flour, and stir until as smooth as it will come, then add 1½ cups of milk and 1 teaspoon of caramel or soup-browning, and season highly with salt and pepper. Put the chestnuts in the sauce, and fill pastry cases with the mixture.

PATTIES OF FRESH GREEN PEAS

Use fresh green peas boiled as directed, or use canned French peas; reheat in white sauce, and use to fill patties or timbale cases. A little finely chopped mint can be added to the sauce if liked.

EGG PATTIES

Hard boil the eggs required, chop fine when cold, and reheat in parsley sauce, and use to fill heated cases or patties, or use eggs Newburg for filling.

MACEDOINE PATTIES

Use imported macedoine of vegetables, heat in a double boiler with white sauce, and use as patty filling in heated cases.

MUSHROOM PATTIES

Cut fresh mushrooms in quarters, toss them in melted butter for five minutes, then cover them with white or brown sauce, and serve in heated cases or patties. Any of the recipes given for mushrooms can be used to fill patty cases, mushrooms Newburg being especially suitable.

CANNED MUSHROOM PATTIES

Toss the mushroom buttons in hot butter for five minutes, cover them with white sauce, and use to fill heated patties.

SAUCES

CARAMEL FOR COLOURING

Put ½ cup of powdered sugar in a small saucepan over a very low fire, stir with a wooden spoon until melted, and continue to stir until it is a rich brown; add 2 cups of *warm* water, and let it simmer for fifteen or twenty minutes, then skim and strain, and bottle for use in giving a rich colour to soups and sauces.

Ready-made vegetable extracts of good dark colour can be bought, and are one of the few things which seem better than the home-made product.

REDUCED VINEGAR

This adds a delicious flavour to many sauces, vegetables, and soups, and is made by putting vinegar, with a little salt and pepper, in a saucepan and letting it boil rapidly until reduced, the proportions being 2 tablespoons of vinegar, 1 saltspoon of salt, and a pinch of pepper cooked until reduced to 1 teaspoon of liquid. Strain before using.

SAUCE BERNAISE

Into 1 tablespoon of reduced vinegar beat slowly the yolks of 4 eggs to which has been added 2 tablespoons of cold water, and when well mixed hold in a small saucepan above a slow fire; put in a small bit of butter, and when melted stir in another, and so continue until 1½ tablespoons have been used. When the sauce is smooth and creamy, season with salt and pepper or paprika, and add ½ teaspoon of tarragon vinegar, or 1 teaspoon of minced tarragon leaves. The sauce cannot be served very hot or it will curdle. It may be served cold also.

BLACK BUTTER SAUCE

Put 3 or 4 tablespoons of butter in a saucepan with 1 saltspoon of salt and a little pepper, and let cook slowly until browned; then add 1 teaspoon of reduced vinegar or lemon juice, and serve hot.

BREAD SAUCE

Put 1 large slice of bread, cut an inch thick, into 2 cups of milk with 1 onion with 4 cloves stuck in it, add pepper, salt, and 1 teaspoon of butter. Let simmer until the bread is quite soft, lift out the onion and cloves, beat well with a fork, and serve. Serve fine golden brown bread crumbs with the sauce, as these belong with it.

BROWN SAUCE

Put 1 tablespoon of butter in a saucepan, and when well browned, remove from fire, add 1 tablespoon of flour, stirring until smooth; then add gradually 1 cup of vegetable stock or milk, and, when all is smooth and well thickened, ½ teaspoon of brown colouring, and salt and pepper. It improves the flavour to let the stock to be used simmer for ten minutes with 1 bay leaf and ½ an onion added to it.

VARIATIONS OF BROWN SAUCE

Add chopped button mushrooms, chopped fried peppers, tiny pearl onions, boiled eggs, etc., to vary brown sauce.

SAUCE BORDELAISE

To 1 cup of brown sauce add 1 teaspoon of grated onion, 3 minced fresh mushrooms (or 1 tablespoon of chopped canned ones), 2 teaspoons of chopped parsley, and salt and pepper. Stir over a slow fire for five minutes before serving.

DRAWN BUTTER

Melt 4 tablespoons of butter, and stir in until smooth 2 tablespoons of flour; then add slowly 2 cups of boiling vegetable stock, 1 teaspoon of salt, and a little cayenne or paprika.

CURRY SAUCE

Put 1 tablespoon of butter in a saucepan, and when melted stir into it 1 large onion chopped fine, and let simmer for six or seven minutes; then add 1 sour apple chopped fine (or, if it can be had, 1 tablespoon of tamarind chutney), stir for three or four minutes, then add ½ cup of strong vegetable stock or water, and let cook gently for five minutes; pour on another ½ cup of vegetable stock and 1 cup of milk, into which 1 dessert spoon of curry powder has been stirred until smooth; let all boil up once, then press through a sieve, pressing well to get the juices, return to the fire, and to thicken, use 1 tablespoon of flour blended with 1 tablespoon of butter to every cup of liquid. Stir until the consistency of thick cream, and add a little salt before serving. The quantity of curry powder here named will make a mild curry sauce.

CAPER SAUCE

Put 1 tablespoon of butter in a frying pan, and when melted add 1 tablespoon of flour and stir until smooth. Now add, a little at a time, 2 cups of vegetable broth, and stir until it boils and is smooth. Put in 2 heaping tablespoons of capers and 1 chopped hard-boiled egg, and season well with salt and pepper. One tablespoon of cream may be added at the last to enrich the sauce if desired.

CHEESE SAUCE

Make 1 cup of highly seasoned white sauce, and add to it 1 scant cup of grated cheese; stir in a double boiler until the cheese is melted, then add a few drops of yellow colouring extract, and salt and paprika.

FRENCH CUCUMBER SAUCE

Grate 1 cucumber and drain it well, then add to it ½ teaspoon of salt, a dash of cayenne, and 1 tablespoon of vinegar.

DUTCH BUTTER

To every tablespoon of melted butter add 1 teaspoon of lemon juice; season with salt.

DEVILLED SAUCE

Put 1 tablespoon of butter in a saucepan, and when melted add 1 tablespoon of chopped onion, and let cook slowly for five minutes. Then add 1 tablespoon of chopped parsley, 2 tablespoons of vinegar, 1 tablespoon of walnut or mushroom catsup, 1 tablespoon of English mustard, ½ teaspoon of salt, 1 saltspoon of black pepper, and a little cayenne. Thicken with 1 tablespoon of flour, and when smooth add enough vegetable stock to make the consistency of cream. The sauce may be used as it is or pressed through a sieve to strain.

FRENCH SAUCE

Rub together 1 tablespoon of flour and 1 of butter, and put in a saucepan; as it melts add slowly 1 cup of boiling water or vegetable stock, let boil, stirring constantly, then remove from the fire, and when somewhat cooled add the juice of 1 lemon, 2 tablespoons of tarragon or chervil vinegar, 2 egg-yolks slightly beaten, and salt and pepper.

GERMAN SAUCE

Make brown sauce, add ½ can halved button mushrooms and 1 tablespoon of reduced vinegar, and season with salt and pepper.

GERMAN EGG SAUCE

Mix 3 beaten egg-yolks with 1 teaspoon of flour, 1 scant cup of cream or milk, 1 tablespoon of butter, and 1 tablespoon of lemon juice, season with salt and pepper, and beat vigorously, until thickened, over a hot fire, but do not let the sauce boil at all. Add 1 hard-boiled egg, chopped fine, and 1 tablespoon of minced parsley before serving.

EGG SAUCE

To 1 cup of well-made white sauce add 2 hard-boiled eggs chopped fine, and 1 teaspoon of chopped parsley, and a little salt and paprika.

HERB SAUCES

Make a good white sauce and to each 2 cups of sauce add the herbs selected, prepared as follows: Take a handful of the leaves, and after washing them well put them in a pan with a little salted boiling water; let cook for five minutes, then drain, and dry with a cloth, and put in a mortar with 1 tablespoon of butter, and macerate until fine; add this to the white sauce. In this way parsley, mint, tarragon, chervil, and other herb sauces can be made.

SAUCE HOLLANDAISE

To 1 tablespoon of reduced vinegar add the yolks of 4 eggs mixed with 2 tablespoons of cold water; stir well together, and cook by holding above a very slow fire, in order to prevent curdling; add 2 tablespoons of butter, stirring it in a little at a time until all is used. Season with salt and pepper and serve warm or cold.

HORSE-RADISH SAUCE

Rub together 1 tablespoon of butter and 1 of flour and put in a saucepan. When melted and smooth from stirring, add slowly 1½ cups of heated milk; when properly thickened by slow cooking, put in 3 tablespoons of grated horse-radish, stir well, season with salt, add 1 teaspoon of butter, and serve on croquettes, etc.

MAÎTRE D'HÔTEL SAUCE

This is made by using sauce Hollandaise and adding to it 1 tablespoon of lemon juice and 1 tablespoon of finely chopped parsley.

MINT SAUCE

Wash the mint and take ½ cup of the leaves; chop them fine, macerate in a mortar, then cover with 1 cup of hot vinegar, add 1 teaspoon of sugar, and let stand a few moments before using.

MUSHROOM SAUCE

Make brown sauce and add to it ½ can of button mushrooms, halved. Let heat through before serving.

NUT SAUCES

For these use pignola (pine) nuts, almonds, chestnuts, or any other sort. Remove the shells, blanch in boiling water to remove the inner skin, and chop them very fine. Put 1 tablespoon of butter in a frying pan, and when melted add to it 1 tablespoon of chopped onion, and let cook for five minutes; then add ½ cup of chopped nuts and stir until brown, scrape the contents of the pan into a mortar, and pound them well. Blend 1 tablespoon of flour and 1 tablespoon of butter, put in a saucepan, and when melted and smooth add ½ cup of milk and ½ of the nuts; let cook slowly two or three minutes, add another ½ cup of milk and the remaining nuts. Salt well, and add a little pepper; let cook very slowly, and when the sauce is the proper thickness stir in 1 tablespoon of thick cream.

The sauce can be darkened with brown colouring, or by browning the thickening flour in butter.

ONION SAUCE

Chop 4 onions very fine and brown them in 3 tablespoons of butter; add 1 tablespoon of flour, let this brown also, and thin with 1 cup of broth or water or milk. Add pepper and salt, and beat 1 egg-yolk into it before serving. Serve either strained or unstrained.

PARSLEY BUTTER

Put butter in a saucepan, and when melted add finely chopped parsley and some salt, using 1 teaspoon of parsley to every tablespoon of butter used. Serve on boiled potatoes, asparagus, etc.

PARSLEY SAUCE

Into 2 cups of white sauce stir 1 beaten egg and 2 tablespoons of finely chopped parsley.

SAUCE PROVENÇAL

To 1 cup of Spanish sauce add 1 tablespoon of white wine, 2 tablespoons of tomato sauce, and 1 tablespoon of chopped chives, and cook together slowly ten minutes before serving. Season with salt and pepper before serving.

PIQUANT SAUCE

Put 4 tablespoons of vinegar in a saucepan with 1 tablespoon of chopped shallots or onions, and let cook slowly until only 1 tablespoon remains; add to this 1 cup of Spanish sauce, and when at boiling point put in the sauce 2 teaspoons of minced sour pickles, 1 teaspoon of chopped parsley, and some salt and pepper; serve with croquettes or vegetables.

SAUCE RAVIGOTE

Ravigote is merely the name applied to the mixture of herbs combined with flavouring for this sauce. These are chives, cress, burnet and chervil, in equal proportions. Use 2 tablespoons of the mixed herbs, scald them in tarragon vinegar, drain them, chop them fine, and add them to 1 cup of plain mayonnaise.

SAUCE ROBERT

This is made by adding to 1 cup of Spanish sauce 2 tablespoons of white wine, 1 teaspoon of onion juice, and 1½ teaspoons of mustard mixed with 2 teaspoons tarragon vinegar. Season, and make hot in a double boiler, letting all cook slowly together ten minutes.

SPANISH SAUCE

This is a rich sauce which is used as a basis for many sauces, and can be made at a leisure time and used any time within a few days. Any stock in which vegetables have been cooked may be used, but the best one is made as follows: Wash 4 or 5 cups of red beans or lentils, and after soaking them in 2 quarts of water for ten hours or more empty them with the same water into a saucepan, and put with them 3 onions halved, 3 sprigs of parsley, 1 cup of carrots quartered, ½ cup of diced turnips, 1 tablespoon of salt, 2 stalks of celery cut in short lengths, and a small bag containing 1 teaspoon of thyme, 2 bay leaves, 6 cloves, 6 whole peppers, and 1 teaspoon of allspice berries. Let boil hard for one minute, then set on the stove where it will simmer slowly for two hours. Strain the broth through a fine sieve, and use the vegetables in a stew, a deep pie, or a curry. To finish the Spanish sauce put 2 tablespoons of butter in a saucepan, and when melted stir into it 2 tablespoons of flour and let brown, stirring constantly; then add a little stock at a time until about 2 cups have been used and the sauce is the consistency of thick cream. Darken with 1 teaspoon of brown colouring, add 1 tablespoon of sherry, and pepper and salt.

SPINACH SAUCE

Put 1 cup of freshly cooked or canned spinach, from which the juice has been pressed, into a basin or mortar, and chop or mash to a pulp. Melt 1 tablespoon of butter in a saucepan, add to it 1 small onion chopped fine, let cook slowly for five minutes, then add the spinach, and let cook for ten minutes more. Put 1 cup of milk into a double boiler with 1 bay leaf, 1 stalk of celery (or some celery seed), and when it boils add 1 tablespoon of flour blended with 1 tablespoon of butter; season with salt and pepper, and when thickened stir the spinach into this, sprinkle with grated nutmeg, and let cook together for ten minutes. Press through a sieve before serving.

SAUCE TARTARE

Make a plain mayonnaise sauce (see Salads), and to each cup add 1 teaspoon of gherkins and 2 teaspoons of capers, both very finely minced; sprinkle a little cayenne on the sauce before serving.

TOMATO SAUCE

Use 6 fresh tomatoes, and after washing them slice them, skins and all. Put 1 tablespoon of butter in a saucepan, and when melted add 2 tablespoons of finely chopped onion, let cook slowly for five minutes, then put with them the tomatoes, 2 bay leaves, 1 clove of garlic, 1 teaspoon of sugar, some pepper and salt, and let cook gently for fifteen minutes; then strain, pressing through a sieve, and return the liquid to the fire to simmer until reduced to the proper consistency.

TOMATO SAUCE WITH OTHER VEGETABLES

Make tomato sauce, using with it chopped celery, chopped peppers, or chopped mushrooms, which have been fried for ten minutes in hot butter and added after the sauce is strained.

WHITE SAUCE

Put 2 tablespoons of butter in a saucepan, and as soon as it is melted stir into it slowly 3 tablespoons of flour, using 1 tablespoon at a time, then add slowly 2 cups of warm vegetable stock or milk, stirring all the while; then add ⅔ of a teaspoon of salt, 1 saltspoon of pepper, and cook slowly for five minutes, stirring constantly; add 1 tablespoon of butter, and stir for another minute. Some flour thickens more than others, and if the sauce seems too thick, thin with a little cream or milk.

White sauce may be varied in many ways by using onion juice, mushroom catsup, chopped chives, etc.

The white sauce may be made in a double boiler. Put the milk in the top receptacle, and when boiling add the flour dissolved in a little cold milk, then the butter, etc., and let cook ten minutes or until thickened.

SAUCE VINAIGRETTE

To each cup of French dressing add 1 tablespoon of minced onion and 1 tablespoon of macerated parsley.

TOMATO SAUCE WITH NUTS

Chop 2 tablespoons of blanched nuts, fry them for ten minutes in 1 tablespoon of melted butter, and add these to strained tomato sauce.

TOMATO SAUCE WITH EGG

To each cup of strained tomato sauce add 2 hard-boiled eggs chopped fine.

EGG DISHES

BOILED EGGS

Eggs are very palatable when put in boiling water and cooked for three or three and a half minutes, but some cooks recommend that "boiled eggs" should never boil, but instead, be placed in a large saucepan which is filled with water that has boiled and just been removed from the fire. The instructions are to cover the saucepan closely after putting the eggs in the water, and let it stand on the back of the stove, the eggs to be removed in ten minutes if wanted soft, and in twenty minutes if liked well set. Hard-boiled eggs are certainly more palatable cooked in this way than when boiled for ten minutes in the ordinary way.

FRIED EGGS

Put a little butter into a small frying pan, and when melted break an egg into a saucer, and slide it carefully into the hot butter, and let it fry until the white is thoroughly set, cooking as many as are required, separately, in the same way. If a tight cover is put over the frying pan when the egg is put in, the yolk of the egg will be as pink as a nicely poached egg when done. Season with pepper and salt before serving. A little Worcestershire sauce or walnut catsup heated in the pan and poured over fried eggs adds variety.

POACHED EGGS

Fill a deep frying pan ⅔ full of hot water, and stir into it one teaspoon of vinegar and 1 teaspoon of salt. When the water reaches boiling point break the eggs carefully one by one into it, remove the pan from the intense heat, cover it, and let the eggs cook until the whites are firmly set. If the water is shallow the eggs will spread and be more flat, in which case the boiling water must be dipped up over the yolks with a spoon to make them pink; if the water is deep the eggs will be more round than flat. When the eggs are done lift them carefully from the water with a perforated strainer in order to drain off the water thoroughly, and serve them on hot toast.

POACHED EGGS WITH GRAVY

Poach eggs and serve them with Sauce Bernaise, or any piquant sauce.

POACHED EGGS INDIENNE

Poach the number of eggs required, and after placing them on toast pour over them a thin curry sauce.

EGGS WALDORF

Place nicely poached eggs on toast, and fit a freshly cooked mushroom as a cap over each yolk. Surround the toast with brown sauce containing quartered mushrooms.

SCRAMBLED EGGS

Break six or more into a bowl, beat them lightly with a fork, and pour them into a frying pan into which 1 tablespoon of butter has been melted; stir continually over a very slow fire until they are well set, seasoning them meanwhile with pepper and salt, and adding another ½ tablespoon of butter in small pieces during the cooking. Serve with a garnish of small triangular pieces of toast. One tablespoon of cream can be added to the eggs before serving if desired. Eggs may be scrambled with milk, using ½ cup of milk to 4 eggs, and then proceeding as above.

SCRAMBLED EGGS WITH CHEESE

Make plain scrambled eggs, and when nearly set add 2 tablespoons of grated cheese for every 6 eggs used, and 1 tablespoon of chopped parsley. Serve on toast.

SCRAMBLED EGGS WITH MUSHROOMS, PEAS, ETC.

Scramble 6 eggs, and two or three minutes before removing from the fire add to them a can of button mushrooms cut in slices, lengthwise, and 1 tablespoon of finely chopped parsley. In the same way peas, tomatoes, asparagus tips, chopped sweet peppers, etc., can be used.

SAVOURY SCRAMBLED EGGS

Prepare plain scrambled eggs, and just before taking off the fire add 2 tablespoons of chopped chives (or green stems of young onions or shallots can be used instead), and ½ a tablespoon of finely chopped parsley; serve on hot toast.

SCRAMBLED EGGS INDIENNE

Make plain scrambled eggs, and just before serving stir into them 1 tablespoon of cream, into which has been stirred 1 teaspoon of curry powder and ½ teaspoon of onion juice. Serve on hot toast.

SPANISH EGGS

For 6 eggs use 1 large tomato and 1 small onion. Chop the onion fine, and fry it five minutes in 1 tablespoon of butter; then add the chopped tomato, and stir another minute over the fire. Now pour in the eggs and scramble them, adding 1 teaspoon of salt and a saltspoon of pepper. Garnish with small triangles of toast.

SHIRRED EGGS

Butter individual gratin dishes, and break into them 1 or 2 eggs as desired. Season with salt and pepper, and a sprinkling of finely chopped parsley, and put into the oven for five minutes, or until the eggs are set. Place each dish on a small plate with a paper doily.

SHIRRED EGGS WITH TOMATOES

Use as many shallow, individual gratin dishes as there are persons to be served, and, after buttering each dish, break into it 1 egg, taking care not to break the yolk. Halve some small tomatoes, and set one half, cut side up, in each dish; season the whole with pepper and salt, and set in the oven for ten minutes or less.

GRIDDLED EGGS

Heat a griddle and butter it slightly, and break upon it 3 or 4 eggs, disturbing the yolks so as to break them. When a little browned on one side turn them with a cake-turner and fry the other side.

PLAIN OMELET

Put 3 or 4 eggs in a bowl and beat them ten or twelve times with a fork vigorously. Put 1 scant tablespoon of butter in a frying pan, and as soon as melted turn in the eggs and shake over a slow fire until they are set; season with salt and pepper, turn the omelet together as it is let to slide from the pan, and place on a hot dish. Make several small omelets rather than one large one, and place on white paper doilies, and garnish with parsley to serve. The trick of shaking an omelet is the secret of making a good one, and the egg mixture should be not over ½ an inch deep in the pan.

OMELET SOUFFLÉ

Take 4 to 6 fresh eggs, separate the yolks and whites, and beat each until as light as possible. Butter a deep frying pan, mix the yolks and whites lightly together with a fork, and put in the hot frying pan, smoothing somewhat with a fork to level. Season the top with pepper and salt, and shake over a slow fire until the omelet is delicately browned on the bottom; turn it together and serve on a hot platter.

HERB OMELET

Make like plain omelet, stirring with every 4 eggs used 1 teaspoon each of powdered thyme, or sweet marjoram, sage, chopped onion tops or chives, and parsley.

CHEESE OMELET

For omelet soufflé made with 6 eggs add ¼ cup of grated cheese to the yolks of the eggs, and ¼ cup to the beaten whites before putting them together.

In making plain omelet with cheese add ¼ cup of cheese to 4 eggs after they are in the omelet pan. Sprinkle with grated cheese to serve, and garnish with watercress or parsley.

RUM OMELET

Make an omelet soufflé, put on a hot dish, and pour ½ cup of heated rum around it, and light it with a match. Rum is easily made to blaze if a teaspoon is filled with it and a lighted match held under the tip of the spoon. The rum on the platter can then be easily lighted with that in the spoon.

BAKED OMELET SOUFFLÉ

Beat the whites of 6 eggs very stiff and the yolks of 3. Mix the whites and the yolks, using a fork; then stir in the juice of half a lemon and 3 tablespoons of powdered sugar. Heap in a buttered baking dish, and cook in a hot oven about fifteen minutes.

EGGS CARMELITE

Prepare 1 cup of very finely chopped boiled spinach by adding to it 1 teaspoon of butter and 1 saltspoon of grated nutmeg, and put where it will keep warm. Hard boil 6 or 8 eggs, then cut each carefully in two, lengthwise; remove the yolks and stir them into the spinach, mashing them well, and mashing all together until the yolks are thoroughly mixed with the spinach; then season with salt and pepper and neatly fill the halves of the whites of the eggs with the spinach. Make a sauce with 2 cups of milk, 1 teaspoon of butter, and 2 tablespoons of flour, a dash of paprika, and 1 cup of grated cheese. When this has thickened arrange 2 or 3 halved eggs in each individual gratin dish, and pour around them some of the sauce, and set in the oven five minutes to make thoroughly hot, or serve on a large dish garnished with small triangular pieces of toast.

EGG WITH MASHED POTATO

Use a long, narrow gratin dish, and arrange cold mashed potato in it in ridges with a spoon, and make three or four hollows in the surface. Into each of these break an egg, and let all bake in the oven until the eggs are set. Tomato or white sauce can be served with this.

EGGS NEWBURG

Hard boil 6 eggs, plunge them into cold water for a moment, then peel, and when cooled, so they will not crumble in cutting, cut them in half. Have ready a sauce made of 1 cup of cream (or milk) and 3 tablespoons of butter, to which when hot is added 2 tablespoons of sherry, 2 tablespoons of brandy (the latter may be omitted), 1 saltspoon of pepper, and 1 teaspoon of salt. Let cook three minutes, then beat in vigorously the beaten yolks of 4 eggs, stir until thickened, add a dash of paprika, and serve over the hard-boiled eggs on toast.

EGGS LYONNAISE

Put 2 tablespoons of butter in a frying pan, and when melted add 1 finely chopped onion, and let simmer slowly for eight or ten minutes; then add 1 tablespoon of flour, and stir well until smooth. Add to this ½ cup of milk, ½ teaspoon of salt, and ½ saltspoon of pepper, and let cook three or four minutes only. Pour into a deep gratin dish, and break upon it 6 eggs; sprinkle with ½ cup of bread crumbs, and let cook in a moderate oven about five minutes, or until the eggs are set. Serve in the same dish.

JAPANESE EGGS

Hard boil the number of eggs required, and, after halving them, remove the yolks, and mix them with a little butter (using 1 tablespoon to 6 eggs), pepper, salt, and a little tomato chutney or Harvey sauce. Refill the halved whites with this, and use the eggs to garnish 2 cups of boiled rice. Pour over all 1 cup of white sauce or parsley sauce to serve.

GOLDEN ROD EGGS

Hard boil 5 eggs, take off the shell, and separate the yolks from the whites, chopping the whites fine and pressing the yolks through a sieve, keeping whites and yolks separate. Put 1 cup of milk in a double boiler, and when it boils add to it 1 tablespoon of butter and 1 tablespoon of cornstarch which have been rubbed together, and when the sauce has thickened season it generously with pepper and salt, and stir into it the chopped whites of the eggs. While the sauce is cooking prepare 5 rounds of toast, and place them on a hot dish. Cover each piece of toast with a layer of white sauce, sprinkle this with a layer of the yolks, then more of the white sauce, and the remainder of the yolks, season with salt and pepper, and stand in the oven a moment or two before serving.

FROTHED EGGS

Separate the yolks and whites of as many eggs as are required, putting each yolk in its shell or in a separate dish. Beat the whites until very stiff, and fill a well-buttered custard cup half full of the white of egg; make a hole in the centre, sprinkle with salt, pepper, and lemon juice, and drop a yolk in each cup. Put in a shallow pan of boiling water with a cover on it, and when the eggs are set turn out onto buttered toast. Garnish with parsley butter.

FRIED STUFFED EGGS

Hard boil 6 eggs and halve them carefully, removing the yolks. Put the yolks through a sieve, and rub to a paste with 1 tablespoon of melted butter, salt, pepper, and ¼ cup of cream or milk, using a little at a time, so as not to use it all unless needed to make the mixture of the right consistency for refilling the halved whites. Carefully fill the places made vacant by the removed yolks, roll the half-egg in beaten egg and crumbs, and fry in deep, hot fat. Serve with 2 cups of white sauce, and add to it 2 tablespoons of diced pickled beets, which makes the sauce pink.

This same effect may be had to some extent by simply using hard-boiled eggs, frying them, and serving with same sauce or white sauce, to which 1 tablespoon of capers has been added.

SWISS EGG TOAST

Melt 1 tablespoon of butter on a shallow or flat dish, and sprinkle over it 1½ tablespoons of grated cheese; then break into the butter 3 eggs, taking care not to break the yolks. Sprinkle well with salt and pepper and 1½ tablespoons of grated cheese mixed with 2 teaspoons of finely chopped parsley. Bake in the oven until the eggs are set, then cut each egg out round with a cutter, and serve on rounds of toast.

DEVILLED EGGS

Hard boil the number of eggs required, halve them, and serve on toast with devilled sauce.

EGGS CAROLINA

To serve four persons hard boil 6 eggs, then put them in cold water for one minute, peel 2 of them, chop the whites, and mix with melted butter and 1 tablespoon of chopped parsley, and form into nests on 4 pieces of hot "corn bread." Then peel the other 4 eggs, and arrange one on end in each nest. Pour a little parsley butter on each, and season with salt and pepper.

MÜNCHNER EGGS

Hard boil 6 eggs, then peel them, and put each on a leaf of lettuce or cabbage, encircling it with grated horse-radish, and serve with a sauce made of vinegar to which is added salt and dry mustard.

EGGS IN MARINADE

Hard boil the eggs required, then remove the shells, and stick 4 cloves in each egg. Put 2 cups of vinegar on to boil, and rub together a little vinegar, ½ teaspoon of mustard, ½ teaspoon of salt, and ½ teaspoon of pepper, and stir into the boiling vinegar. Place the eggs in a glass jar, and pour the boiled vinegar over them. They can be used in a fortnight, halved or sliced as a garnish or in salads.

EGGS PARISIENNE

Butter as many timbale moulds as are required, and dust the inside with chopped parsley; then break into each an egg, and sprinkle with salt and pepper. Set the moulds in water in a shallow pan, and place in the oven until well set or hard. Turn out onto a flat dish, or on individual dishes, and with them serve bread sauce, or any sauce desired.

EGGS PERIGORD

Butter small moulds or cups, then sprinkle them with chopped parsley, and on the bottom (which will be the top when they are turned out) place a symmetrical pattern made of cut beets and truffles or pickled walnuts. Drop one egg into each mould, dredge with salt and pepper, and set the moulds in a pan of boiling water; cover, and let cook until firm. Turn out onto rounds of toast, and serve with a hot tomato sauce, or any savoury sauce.

EGGS WITH CHEESE

Into a shallow round or oval gratin dish, or small individual dishes, put melted butter to cover the bottom, and encircle the outer edge with thinly sliced, rather dry, cheese; inside this break enough eggs to cover the bottom of the dish, taking care not to break the yolks. Season with salt and pepper, and put into the oven until the whites of the eggs are thoroughly set.

EGGS MORNAY

Drop eggs into a buttered baking dish, and then cover them with a highly seasoned white sauce to which some egg-yolks have been added (using 1 yolk to each ½ cup of sauce), also salt and paprika. Sprinkle the top with grated cheese, and put in the oven to bake until the egg is firmly set.

CREAMED EGGS

Butter a shallow dish, pour into it 1 scant cup of milk, and let heat. When hot cover the surface with eggs, cover, and let poach on top of stove until set; sprinkle with celery salt, and then cover with cream, and set in the oven for five minutes. Sprinkle the top with finely chopped celery tops to serve. This may be cooked in one large dish or in individual gratin dishes.

EGGS OMAR PASHA

Butter individual gratin dishes, and break 2 eggs into each, taking care not to break the yolks. Slice small onions so the separate rings are unbroken, and place a circle of these rings on the eggs around the edge of the dish. Sprinkle with salt and pepper, then with grated cheese, and bake in a slow oven until the eggs are thoroughly set.

TURKISH EGGS

Butter one large gratin dish or several small ones, break into them enough eggs to cover the bottom, taking care not to break the yolks; put them in a moderate oven until the whites are quite set, and then garnish by putting a few tablespoons of boiled rice on the eggs around the edge of the dish, alternating with button mushrooms, which have been cut in thin slices and mixed with brown sauce. Season with salt and pepper just before serving.

EGGS BEURRE-NOIR

These are best served in individual gratin dishes measuring about four inches across. Put 2 tablespoons of butter in a saucepan, and let it cook over a slow fire until a rich brown, but not burnt. Add to it 1 teaspoon of lemon juice, and cover the bottom of each gratin dish with the (black) butter; then break into each dish 1 egg, or 2 if required, taking care not to break the yolk. Season with salt and pepper and arrange 8 or 10 capers on each; put in the oven eight or ten minutes, or until the eggs are well set. Set each dish on a doily on a small plate before serving, with a sprig of parsley on the side.

EGGS CREOLE

Take a shallow gratin dish large enough to contain the eggs required, allowing 2 eggs to each person, butter the gratin dish, and break the eggs carefully into it, taking care not to break the yolks; season with pepper and salt, and set in a moderate oven until the whites are stiff; while they are cooking prepare the following garnish which will be sufficient for 6 or 8 eggs. Put 1 tablespoon of butter in a saucepan; when melted add 1 onion cut into thin slices, and stir it about three or four minutes. Then add to it 1 tomato which has been peeled and chopped, 1 sweet green pepper cut in very thin slices, each broken in several pieces, and ½ can of button mushrooms, which are prepared by draining and washing and cutting lengthwise in 3 or 4 pieces. Let all cook slowly together for eight or ten minutes, stirring carefully and adding more butter if necessary. When nearly cooked season generously with pepper and salt, add 1 tablespoon of tomato sauce, and when the eggs are removed from the oven place this garnish on the eggs, encircling the outer edge. This garnish can be varied as to quantities to suit taste, using more or less tomatoes or onions. This is very nice done in individual gratin dishes, 2 eggs being used in each dish.

EGGS IN SAVOURY BUTTER

Savoury butter is made by melting good butter, and adding to it any chopped herb,— chives, parsley, etc. Put a little of this in individual gratin dishes, and break into them 1 or 2 eggs as desired. Pour a little of the savoury butter over the top of each egg, season with salt and pepper, and put in the oven until the eggs are thoroughly set. If fresh tarragon is available, two nicely shaped leaves crossed on the yolk of the egg make a pretty garnish, or two leaves of lemon verbena may be used instead.

EGG MOULD FOR VEGETABLES

Make egg mixture as for egg timbales, and pour into a buttered ring mould. Cook in pan of water in the oven twenty minutes or until set, and then turn out onto a hot, round, flat dish, and fill the centre with hot button mushrooms which are mixed with tomato sauce, or with peas, either with or without the sauce.

CANUCK EGG TOAST

Sprinkle fresh toast with walnut, mushroom, or any savoury catsup, then heap on it nicely scrambled eggs in which milk has been used, and on top put a generous layer of grated cheese; season with pepper and salt, and put under the oven flame of a gas stove. Let the cheese brown, then remove and garnish the top with slices cut from black pickled walnuts, or a few capers, or with thin strips of pimentos, or chopped chives.

ESCALLOPED EGGS

Hard boil 8 eggs, cut the whites into medium-sized pieces, and press the yolks through a sieve or ricer. Put 1 cup of milk in a double boiler, and with it 1 tablespoon of finely minced onion, shallot, or chives. When the milk boils add to it 1 tablespoon of thickening flour dissolved in a little milk and stir until thickened. Season with ½ teaspoon of salt, ¼ teaspoon of pepper, a dash of paprika, and stir in the riced egg-yolks and the diced whites. Serve in small dishes, or covered with crumbs and browned in the oven, or on rounds of toast. One or 2 sweet green peppers finely chopped vary this dish.

CHEESE RECIPES

CHEESE RAMEKINS

Take 1 cup of bread crumbs and 1 cup of milk, and cook together until smooth; then add 2 tablespoons of melted butter, 1 scant teaspoon of mustard, and 6 tablespoons of grated cheese. Stir over the fire for one minute, then remove, and add salt and cayenne pepper, and the lightly beaten yolks of 2 eggs; afterwards stir in with a fork the whites of the eggs, beaten to a stiff froth. Pour into ramekin dishes, and bake for fifteen minutes in a moderate oven, or cook and serve in a baking dish.

BAKED CHEESE AND BREAD

Soak 1 cup of bread crumbs for two or three minutes in 2 cups of milk, then beat in the yolks of 2 eggs thoroughly beaten, and 1 cup of grated cheese, and lastly the whites of the 2 eggs beaten to a stiff froth. Put into a buttered baking dish, dot the top with butter, sprinkle with bread crumbs, and bake until a light brown, which will be in from twenty minutes to half an hour.

CHEESE FONDU

Put 1 tablespoon of butter in a saucepan, and when melted add 1 cup of milk, or cream if desired, 1 cup of fine bread crumbs, 2 cups of grated cheese, ½ teaspoon of salt, ½ teaspoon of dry mustard, and some cayenne pepper. Stir constantly until well heated through, and then add 2 lightly beaten eggs, and serve on rounds of toast.

CHEESE RELISH

Put 1 cup of milk into a double boiler, season with pepper and salt, and when hot stir in 1 cup of grated cheese, and let cook for five minutes; then add 3 crumbed soda crackers and serve on toast, with a sprinkling of paprika.

CHEESE MÉRINGUES

Beat the whites of 2 eggs to a stiff froth, and stir into them with a fork 2 tablespoons of Parmesan or grated cheese, 2 drops of tabasco, a little salt and paprika; drop 1 tablespoon at a time into hot fat, and fry until brown; then drain and sprinkle with fresh salt and paprika before serving.

CREAMED CHEESE

Make 2 cups of well-seasoned white sauce, add a few drops of golden yellow colouring, stir into it ½ cup of cheese cut into dice (or grated if preferred), and when the cheese is softened and hot serve on rounds of toast and sprinkle with paprika.

CHEESE PANCAKES

Make small pancakes of 1 cup of milk, 1 egg, and enough flour to thicken, and spread them with grated cheese moistened with a little melted butter; sprinkle chopped chives mixed with parsley over the cheese, and a dash of any savoury catsup (if liked), season with salt and pepper, roll the pancakes after cooking, and serve as a savoury or luncheon dish.

COTTAGE CHEESE

Take 2 quarts or more of sour milk or cream, and add to it the same quantity of rapidly boiling water, turn into a straining-bag, and hang up until dry. When ready to use, turn out of the bag and rub until smooth; add a seasoning of salt and pepper and a little sweet cream. Beat until light and serve ice-cold. A little cream can be served to eat upon it, if liked.

This can also be made by heating the sour milk or cream and using no water, but the milk must only be heated enough to separate and not enough to boil.

WELSH RAREBIT

Cut in very small thin pieces 1 pound of American cheese; put it in a chafing-dish and stir until melted, then add 1 teaspoon of mustard, some salt, and slowly stir in ½ a glass of beer or ale, and season with cayenne or paprika just before serving on toast.

BACHELOR'S RAREBIT

Make Welsh rarebit, and five minutes before serving stir into it 1 tablespoon of chopped green peppers and 1 tablespoon of chopped Spanish pimentos.

DELMONICO RAREBIT

Cut in small pieces 1 pound of American cheese, put it in a chafing-dish and stir until melted; then add ½ a glass of beer or ale, some salt and cayenne or paprika, 1 teaspoon dry mustard, the yolk of 1 egg, then the whipped white of the egg, and serve at once on toast. The white of the egg militates against any "stringiness" which is apt to come from cooking certain sorts of cheese. A little milk can be used, if desired, instead of beer.

PINK RAREBIT

Drain 1 can of tomatoes and put them in a saucepan with 1 tablespoon of butter; season them well with pepper and salt, and after they have cooked fifteen or twenty minutes add 1 pound of fresh American cheese cut into thin slices, and stir until melted; season generously with salt and pepper, and serve on rounds of toast.

LIPTAUER CHEESE

Remove the paper from the smallest Neufchâtel cream cheese, which is nearer like real Liptauer than any other that can be had in America, and set it in the centre of a plate; surround it with 1 teaspoon of paprika, ½ teaspoon of salt, a small mustard spoon of French mustard, a piece of fresh butter half the size of the cheese, 2 teaspoons of minced onion, and 1 teaspoon of capers. The "Liptauer" should be blended at the table with a silver knife. Add first the butter, then the capers, then the onion, then the seasoning, and make into a cream. Serve on brown or white bread, or crackers.

ROQUEFORT CHEESE GOURMET

Cream ½ pound of Roquefort cheese with 1 tablespoon of butter and some salt and 1 tablespoon of sherry, and serve on water crackers.

CAMEMBERT CHEESE

A pretty way to serve Camembert cheese is to place the cheese, when removed from its box and paper, on a round paper doily on a large plate, and surround it with a heavy wreath of watercress and radishes cut to look like flowers.

CHEESE "DREAMS"

Cut fresh cheese into thin slices, spread with made mustard, sprinkle with paprika, lay between two trimmed slices of bread, and toast on both sides until nicely browned, using a very slow fire.

GRATED CHEESE

Instead of throwing away bits of dried cheese these should be grated and put in a wide mouthed, covered glass jar.

www.ingramcontent.com/pod-product-compliance
Lightning Source LLC
Chambersburg PA
CBHW081112080526
44587CB00021B/3557